D0166856

BEDSIDE MANNERS

One Doctor's Reflections on

the Oddly Intimate Encounters

Between

Patient and Healer

DAVID WATTS, M.D.

THREE RIVERS PRESS

NEW YORK

Published in the United States by Three Rivers Press, an imprint of the
Crown Publishing Group, a division of Random House, Inc., New York.
www.crownpublishing.com

Three Rivers Press and the Tugboat design are registered trademarks of
Random House, Inc.

Originally published in hardcover in the United States by Harmony Books,
an imprint of the Crown Publishing Group, a division of Random House
Inc., New York, in 2005.

Library of Congress Cataloging-in-Publication Data
Watts, H. David.
Bedside manners : one doctor's reflections on the oddly intimate encounters
between patient and healer / David Watts.—1st ed.
1. Physician and patient—Anecdotes. 2. Medicine—Anecdotes.
3. Physicians—Anecdotes.
[DNLM: 1. Physician-Patient Relations—Personal Narratives.
2. Empathy—Personal Narratives. 3. Physicians—psychology—
Personal Narratives. W62 W359b 2005] I. Title.
R727.3 W38   2005
610.69'6—dc22   2004016241

ISBN-13: 978-1-4000-8052-6
ISBN-10: 1-4000-8052-5

Printed in the United States of America

Design by Lauren Dong

10 9 8 7 6 5 4 3 2

First Paperback Edition

For my patients . . .

. . . and for Joan

You can observe a lot by watching.

—Yogi Berra

CONTENTS

Contents

CONTENTS

PREFACE

Can you tell me a growing-up story?

The request came from my son, Duston, as I was tucking him into bed. I am familiar with this request. He makes it mostly when he is troubled. Maybe another child has said something mean to him. Maybe he's having to deal with the unthinkable idea of war or capital punishment. Growing up is not easy or fair.

Yet what puts things in place for him and makes him feel better is stories, especially about times past. Instinctively he knows that something is to be found there that will teach or reassure or lull. And I realize that by this ritual he will come to know my relatives, living and dead — to know them by how they come alive and speak and drive cars and take apart tractors for him in the late evenings.

I never intended to be a storyteller. I came to writing because I was looking for something. I was in a difficult transition and I wanted to find a way to say what was going on inside me — or maybe just to find out what was there. I was drawn first to poetry because of its traditional subjects: love, loss, longing . . . the complex and rich and sometimes painful interactions of the family . . . There was stuff there to work with.

As I wrote, I became aware of this niggling little tap, tap, tapping on my shoulder. And a voice that said, Shouldn't you write on the subject you know the most about?

I didn't want to write about my work. But I had to admit that medicine had a rich and beautiful language, and there was a music to the words one could get lost in. And there exists within the doctor-patient relationship this rarest of conditions, which gives the people involved permission to engage in instant, profound human interaction. It's like stepping suddenly into a clearing. Even so, writing about medicine was for someone else.

Well, I finally gave in. My first efforts at writing about the doctor-patient relationship sounded more like articles for the *New England Journal of Medicine* than anything remotely related to art. The cold, distancing language of medicine had crept in and locked out feeling. It was not until I became ruthlessly honest in my treatment of my subject and, by the same token, of myself as a doctor that the language of academics disappeared and the music began to return.

The real turning point came when a young violinist with cancer became my patient. Her struggle and her bright spirit were so inspiring that I just had to find where that passion was coming from. Writing about her taught me how to find what lay underneath. Writing about her allowed me to be deeply moved by other patients with other stories.

Life has a certain irony. My grandfather says that sometimes you just have to go where the horse wants you to go. My horse apparently wanted prose, and wanted it to speak of the struggles of doctors and patients.

Then another surprise: The subjects I was attracted to, the ones that had brought me to poetry in the first place, were to be found quite at home within the heart of medicine. And perhaps to greater effect, for here the tension between the professional and the personal, the locus of these strong emotions within the hard reality of medicine, gave them a certain fresh architecture, a scaffolding to hold on to. And as I learned more clearly from writing about it, the office visit, with its urgency and compression, its precise language and powerful emotions, is itself a poetry.

The stories in this book are true. What I wanted most to celebrate by writing them were the wonderful and inspiring qualities of my patients: their courage, their inventiveness, their quirkiness, even the admirable way they are sometimes irascible and defiant. There is wisdom in the particulars of these characters. Like reflections on the surface of a complex gemstone, these sparkles of personality are what makes the medical experience so interesting, so human, and so impossible to predict.

Something happens when we sit down face-to-face in the spirit of mutual trust and talk about vital issues of health and mortality. Lives open up. We see things we had passed by day after day and never recognized about ourselves. Moreover, this information opens out onto balconies of change, sometimes radical ones. I've seen patients go out and divorce their spouses or change their careers based upon what they learn about themselves. Much of the mysterious action of the human spirit comes forth when we finally relinquish our hiding places. That's what this book is about—what we do about our lives when confronted with mortality.

There are situations and syndromes here that, to my knowledge, have not been described before—or at least I had not known about such things: the man who had to stay awake to stave off his demons during endoscopy, the woman who used poetry to get through a frightening procedure, the doctor who made his living saying yes to insurance companies, the doctor who finally learned how to find value caring for a thankless patient . . .

It turns out, as I wrote deeper and deeper into my subject I revealed more and more about myself. That, I guess, is what literature does. Makes us set aside inhibitions. Makes us find a pathway to the interior. "I write the story, the story writes me."

Some of what I wrote was too painful or specific to include here. The doctor-patient relationship is a sacred and fragile covenant. Patients have a right to their privacy. When writing about my patients I have always asked their permission and with rare exception they would say something like, Oh, that's wonderful. Please do. I think they were genuinely honored to be so recognized. Some names I could not remember. Some people I could not find. But I always tried to disguise my subjects well enough so as to honor the unspoken agreement. Some may recognize themselves. Some may only think they do. The circumstance of literature is specific to us all.

Sometimes, writing these stories late at night, I have become weary with pleasure. Sometimes, reading them again brings the pleasure back. There is a wisdom in stories that goes beyond the circumstance of their creation, and there is a comforting sense of continuation and resilience. Perhaps that is what my son has found there. Gratitude, then, to those who have given us their stories, those who taught me what I now know, and made me a better doctor because of it.

My son is asleep. And bless him. I know that he feels safe now, sleeping in a complex world.

He will need more stories. So will I. There is time for this.

PART

ONE

WHITE RABBITS

Frank is in my waiting room, which means I'm going to be spending a lot of time chasing rabbits — little questions he brings on small crumples of paper that skitter around on my desk, issues he's researched on the Internet and gotten emotional about that usually don't have anything to do with his own circumstance. What's worse, he's about to have an operation, which means he's really going to be worked up.

I'm remembering that he's the guy with too many colonoscopies. "Well, something might have gone wrong since the last one," he'll say. True, but mostly not true. Still, you can resist that argument only so long and then you find yourself torquing another scope through the colon.

And it's not a trivial deal. He goes vagal in the mid-transverse colon, drops his blood pressure, looks like the life force is beating it out of town on the lam. We haven't killed him yet, but we may have come pretty close. And it probably doesn't do a lot of good for his oxygen-starved brain cells that his blood turns to molasses like that. Besides, watching him go shocky sends *my* coronaries into spasm.

I made him sign a release before the last one. That was after the cardiologist told him no more colonoscopies until he got his carotid arteries fixed. Even the *S* word, *stroke,* couldn't deter Frank.

I'm not going to have a stroke, he said.

It struck me that he has one set of evaluators for a real disease that could do real harm and another set for the harmless imaginary one.

He wrote a long letter releasing everyone this side of Kansas from any kind of liability connected with colonoscopy. This is a man who knows what he wants even if it doesn't make sense. We did it, but not before I secretly cleared it with the cardiologist. And we survived. All three of us. But I told him no more nonsense until he got a little more blood flow to his critical body parts.

Now the time has come. 'Bout time, I say. The vascular surgeons are ready to ream out his carotids, but he wants to ask me a few questions first. I knew that. And I know what's coming—so here we go.

I understand you can *get* a stroke from this operation.

That's true.

How common is it?

I don't know. Not very common. It's a question you should ask the vascular surgeons.

They don't hold still as long as you do.

Tie them down and ask them. Meanwhile, they don't do the surgery unless the risk of waiting outweighs the risk of the surgery itself. It's a complicated formula, and I'm sure it's only partly accurate, but that's the intent. It has to do with the extent of stenosis.

What's that?

Narrowing.

How narrow is mine?

Ninety percent, both sides.

Is it safe to say it's small?

What's small?

The risk of stroke.

It's small. Smaller than if you didn't have surgery.

How long will I be in the hospital?

Don't know. These days, probably not long.

Three days?

Thereabouts.

I read that they will put me on something to thin my platelets.

Yeah, probably.

What'll that be?

It's up to the cardiologist and the vascular surgeon.

What are the side effects?

And I'm thinking to myself, This is an example of how questions get asked for the sake of asking. Fueled by their own passion, they spring from a point beyond the platform of knowledge. How would I know the side effects if I don't know the drug?

I can't answer that.

A long silence.

The rabbits were moving from one pile to another.

Well, I have some questions about these bor . . . I can never say it.

What?

Sounds in my abdomen.

Borborygmi.

Yeah, that. I keep getting these loud noises.

You always have that.

Yeah, but I don't believe it's normal.

I know you don't believe it's normal, but you've always *been* normal. Every colonoscopy has been normal. We've studied you from teeth to toenails and there's nothing in there. Nothing.

What do you listen for if you think you've got cancer?

Now we've come to it, I thought. This is the root of the multitudinous colonoscopies, the driving force for the unseen locomotive: failure to believe negative data. Failure to temper the fear that something is wrong somewhere.

I am careful to speak the truth. But truth comes in many packages and it looks different to different people. For Frank I will speak it in a way that wants to bring him back to earth. Just somewhere along terra firma. It would be a mistake to lay out all the variables. That would give him too many openings to hang himself on yet another obsessive rope of worry. So I overstate.

You don't have cancer.

How can you be sure?

You don't have cancer. Since he cannot shut that door, I shut it for him.

He acts like he didn't want to hear this. He looks uneasy, fumbling with his notes as if they, by their meticulous preparations, will ride him over this unpleasant hiatus. They do not. He is forced to accept and move on.

Well, what do abnormal bowel sounds sound like?

I could be offended by that question. Layered into it is distrust of my ability, my training and experience to listen and report, as if only he, with his untrained ear, can decide what is normal. I conclude it is an accident of distraction. Of obsession. He is blinded by his worries.

I indulge him; I'm not sure why. But I can feel that I'm getting close to my limit.

Bowel sounds are abnormal if they are absent for one minute in all four quadrants of the abdomen, if they are high-pitched and occur in rushes as they do during a dynamic obstruction, or if they are amphoric, meaning that they sound cavernous, like water dripping in a very wet cave —

He interrupts: Can you be more specific?

No.

No?

No. End of lesson.

Well, I want you to hear —

I've listened to your belly a hundred times.

No, I mean —

And he brings out a little velvet pouch, something you might see holding a family heirloom, a watch perhaps, the lovingly engraved kind, made of gold and wound by a tiny gold key. He lays it on the table and starts clumsily trying to extricate whatever it is that is wedged inside.

And with a straight face he says, I made a recording of these bo . . . bo . . . bobo . . . rygeums, or whatever. I want you to listen to it.

By now he has the recording device out on the table and is fumbling with it, trying to get it to play. It's not cued to the proper place and he is madly forwarding and rewinding. I realize I am most amazed not by the weirdness it takes to record one's own bowel sounds, not by his solipsistic assumption that I will find this of such great and compelling interest as to arrest my whole practice while we await the multimedia presentation, but that I will tolerate his time-consuming fiddlings with this bowel-noise recording device of his while patients fully deserving my attention wait their turn. Were it not so humorous, it would be maddening.

Without thinking, my body has stood up and is leaving the room. I babble something polite like I have to see someone down the hall, and am gone before I can laugh or burst out with something I'd be sorry for. I am tempted to relate this story to those in the hallway, but who would believe that there's a guy in my office playing a recording of his own bowel sounds?

When I return, he's found it. He plays me ten seconds of

static, mike noise, adventitial sounds. And in the background, harmless bowel mumblings.

Normal, I pronounce.

Are you sure?

Sure.

He is incredulous, but I leave him no openings. I am not in the mood for encores.

He is quiet for a moment. Then he rallies. I was reading about fistulae, he says.

Oh no.

Yeah, and how do you know if you've got a fistula?

Frank, I say. Cut it out. You've got a real problem in your carotids and you're out there trying to invent something in your gut you'd rather talk about. We've been there. Done that. Checked you out, first class. All is well in loop-de-loop land.

I have stunned him to silence. Even so, I know I've not heard the last of this. When he is away from me and my slaps in the face of the disease he believes in so furiously he almost wants it, doubts will filter in along the periphery and eventually, because they are welcome there, occupy again the pathways to the center of his being. He will build them up meticulously, like a young man smitten with a model airplane project, with the same concentration and enthusiasm of one whose grand vision is somehow tied to what he is building, all energies now turned in the same direction, recruiting evidence, plotting how to convert the heathens who refuse to see the obvious. Oh, for someone to share his vision.

It's not me, I say.

What?

Frank, go have your surgery. And blessings be upon you. For Christ's sake, just do what you need to do. You'll live longer.

He gathers up his rabbits and tucks them in his pocket. As I watch him, he looks like a man picking up chess pieces at the end of a bad game, not accepting the outcome.

Then he leans over the desk. Can we talk about this again? he says.

THE DOCTOR WITH
FOOD ON HIS SHIRT

He was a doctor with food on his shirt, she said.

You don't like to see that, I said. You don't like to see a doctor with food on his shirt.

And, she said, he put me in a room that wasn't a room but open space with a curtain around it, short as a miniskirt.

You don't like to see that, I said.

He said he didn't know what Asacol was and why I was taking it. I said it was for my disease. He said he didn't know why they gave Asacol for that disease. I said I'd been taking it for years — Hmm, he said — for my disease and I thought that everybody who had this disease took it. He said he noticed that I worked for that company that had the big scandal recently and what did I know about that scandal because he was interested in what did I know about it. And I said I'd rather talk about my disease, which was why I came, to talk about my disease.

You don't like to see that, I said. You don't like to see a doctor who doesn't want to talk about your disease.

And people were walking up and down outside my curtained-off open space, which was not a room, talking loudly about weight-loss pills and which one worked best, and how Josie's boobs really looked a lot better now that she'd got them fixed.

And he asked me a couple of questions which I don't remember, but I do remember it didn't sound like he knew very much about my disease, or maybe nothing at all, because he looked at me and said you look okay, you look okay to work—just like that—and I said aren't you going to examine me and he said okay and put his hand on my belly. But I know you can't tell the color of the colon inside by putting your hand on the belly outside.

He didn't look at the disease, I said.

He didn't look at the disease, she said. He might not have known where to look.

Maybe he's a hired gun, I said.

What do you mean, hired gun?

Maybe he's a paid killer.

What do you mean, paid killer?

I said, Maybe they have paid him to kill off your disability, the disability you paid into, working all those years at that company with the scandal and the days that made your disease worse, and paying in each month to social security and state disability, that money you paid, in case you needed it later and now you need it and they want him to kill it off.

But isn't the system supposed to take care of you? she said. That's what they said when they withheld all that money: The system will care for you when you need it.

I said, It's cheaper for the system to pay a doctor who will file a report to kill off the disability I put you on and that you deserve because your colitis will not stay under control as long as you work for that company, cheaper than it is to pay your disability. It's economics.

She said she could see that and it sure felt that way, but she didn't understand the part about how a doctor could train under that oath to do — what is it? — do no harm? And then go around killing off her disability like that.

I said, Let me tell you a story. Suppose you're a doctor whose practice is not going well and all the patients seem to be going down the street to the doctor who doesn't have any food on his shirt. And every patient who sees *him* is one patient fewer who sees *you*, and you're looking around for some way to pay the overhead and buy a biscuit for breakfast and the disability company sends you a patient with ulcerative colitis who can't work anymore and you look at her and say, She looks like she can work, and they pay you for that. Pay you pretty well. For that. And you keep your office and your biscuit and maybe you know the principle or maybe you don't know the principle, that if you say no to the disability company, they won't be as inclined to send you any more patients, but as long as you keep saying "back to work" and things like that, they will keep you busy.

And she said, Oh.

And then she asked, What did he say in his letter?

And I read her the part about how she looked okay and he didn't see why she couldn't do some work of some kind.

And she didn't say anything.

And I said, You could make an appeal, and she said, That's the kind of stress that makes my disease worse and that I'm trying to avoid by all this, and I said, I understand, and she said, I'll be okay. But I sure could have used some of that money.

I said I was sorry and then something about how you don't like to see things turn out this way, and she said, Thanks, and we sat for a while not saying anything.

And then she said, You know, I found out he's not a gastroenterologist. He's a weight-loss doctor.

And I said, Was he fat?

And she said, Yes he was.

And what kind of food was it, anyway?

And she said, I'm not sure. It might have been tomato. Pizza sauce or something.

And I said, You don't like to see that. You don't like to see a doctor with food on his shirt.

ADVANCE DIRECTIVE

I'd like to be somewhere where the last word of every sentence is not . . . *Okay?*

I laugh.

They're always in a hurry to finish this and be on to that, she says.

I change the subject. You're in pretty good shape for the shape you're in, I say.

By this time I have tracked her down from ICU to the Step-Down Unit, then to the third-floor Radiology Suite. I can feel the pull of the highway that wanted to take me home thirty minutes ago. I am in no mood for delicate conversation. I am speaking to an eighty-five-year-old woman, lying on the X-ray table, her face still swollen with infection and antibiotics.

It is her turn to laugh. You have strange taste in women, she says.

I like feisty ones, I say.

And I know the issue: She's just off the operating table for a perforated gastric ulcer. She has a big infection at the surgical site and has been refusing the central IV catheter that would give her nourishment, saying she just wanted to be left alone. Meanwhile, the prospect of another surgery looms.

At the ethics meeting yesterday they worried she wasn't competent to make the heavy decisions of life and death.

I'm disappointed, she says.

Why?

Don't you have a copy of my advance directives?

Yeah, but you didn't die. Your directives say that if your heart stops or you quit breathing we do nothing. But you didn't do that.

Too bad, she says.

And it brought us up square against the same old puzzle we struggle and struggle with but never solve. How can we? Here's an old lady with a quirky, offbeat sense of humor who chides the medical system for being so impertinent as to cross the street before checking the traffic light. What appears to be confusion might just be the outspoken rantings of her seasoned personality.

It reminds me of my mother's Winnie-the-Pooh form of understated intelligence, and how it disguised her competency in later years.

Are you competent? I ask.

Hell, yes.

Sounds good to me, I say.

What do *you* think I should do? she says. What if I need surgery again?

Well, you're pretty healthy, I say. Just a little crabby.

She frowns.

But I take that as a good sign.

So you think I should do it?

She's pinning me down, the old goat. Well, here we go.

There are three possible outcomes, I say. Two of them good.

Which two?

The first is easy: getting better. The others, staying the same or dying . . . well . . . for this I have to go back to what *she's* thinking.

The house staff said you were about ready to give up and check out, I say.

Maybe I was.

Time to push her a little. Well if that's so, not making it through surgery is a good outcome.

Possibly. But what do you think?

I can't answer that. All I can say is that if it were me lying on this table knowing what I know about *my* life, I'd have to go for it.

I expect a pause, a pondering, a rebuttal that says my life is not her life. But she bounces right back.

I'll do it, she says.

Let's be sure about this, I say. It seems we got to home plate a little fast. Does that mean they can start an IV?

Yeah.

Put in a feeding line?

Yeah.

Do surgery if it is required?

If it is required.

The orderlies come to wheel her back to the floor. She compliments them on how deftly they shift her to the gurney. Something has passed between us that feels like a clean base hit.

I turn to write the note in the chart that will signal her change of heart, and I wonder what the ethics committee would say.

Yes, I know all about competency testing. But that only tells us about the brain. The brain informs, but it's the heart that makes decisions.

And her heart? Medically, it's great. After all, it has survived this ordeal. But spiritually?

I don't know if the decision we've made is right. But for her, and for me, and for the moment in which it was made, it was perfect.

SYLVESTER

Have you ever sewn anybody up?

Your first night in the ER, you want *not* to be noticed. A medical student in the ER is like an acolyte with a passport to the Basilica, accepted in the circle of the holy, keeping his ignorance under his vestments.

It was the resident who had asked, a Ben Casey, no-nonsense-type guy, all hair and body odor under his green scrubs.

The intensity of his eyes required a quick and precise answer.

No, I said.

Then come with me.

The resident pulled a chart—a clipboard with its billowing pages of paper—from the slot at the end of the triage desk and handed it to me.

Read it, he commanded.

I didn't know where to begin, so I stumbled through name, date . . .

No, no, not that stuff. The chief complaint.

I looked at the line marked CC.

Laceration, scalp, I said.

What else?

Hit on the head with a bar stool. Said the guy just walked up and hit him for no reason. Brought in by police.

Fine. He's yours. Call me when you get him in a room.

The resident disappeared as if possessed by his next location.

Before I had time to struggle with the idea of where the "room" was and what I was supposed to do when I got there, an ER nurse whizzed by and locked arms with me, and I found myself suddenly traveling like an echo down the terrazzo corridor to the waiting room.

Babies were crying, couples were holding on to each other . . . we seemed to have entered Albert Schweitzer's holding area at Lambaréné. I was in the presence of misery, collective suffering on a scale I'd not seen before. Eyes rose to look at me — dispassionately, I thought, as if surveying intentions I could not even know myself — at my starched white student's jacket with its shiny, hardly used Littman stethoscope curled crisply in the top pocket, my blue-and-white name tag, the book of diagnostic signs in my side pocket like a virginal peripheral brain, and the discomfort welling up like magma inside me.

Sylvester! The nurse shouted from a point that must have been two millimeters from my ear.

A tall, lanky, kind-faced black man I hadn't noticed before stood and, clasping a bloodstained handkerchief to the dome of his head, faltered forward.

That's me, he said.

Immediately we were in a treatment room, washed in a quality of light that penetrated every dark thing. Sylvester was lying on the table, head covered with orange suds — a mix of Betadine and blood and smutty Wildroot Cream-Oil — that dripped in a foamy collective, noiselessly, to the floor. The nurse, in her gloves, was scrubbing him into a froth.

Here, she said, handing me a saline sponge. Get your feet wet.

I reached for the sponge.

She drew it back. Wait, she said. Take off your coat, get on a gown, and glove up. What size do you wear?

I had no idea. She looked at my hands and pointed to the bin marked Large. Try these.

I scrubbed.

And because I suddenly remembered, I said, The resident said to call when we got —

The nurse just smiled. Scrub, she said. Five more minutes. And then — she placed a disposable razor on the Mayo stand — shave a two-centimeter margin around the laceration. I've got to start an IV next door, but I'll be back.

Odor was rising from Sylvester's body. It was a mix of

beer and armpit sweat and yeast and Granger roll-your-own cigarette tobacco. And now Betadine, too.

Does it hurt? I asked.

Naw, he said.

Just let me know.

I scrubbed and shaved and scrubbed some more. So who got you? I asked. I was embarrassed by the obvious curiosity of the question, a detail that should not be important to a compassionate and experienced helper. But I was new and I was interested in everything.

My friend, he said.

The nurse came back, sloshed the wound with sterile saline.

Irrigation, she said, and sloshed until it lay gaping and exposed before us. It was jagged at one end, with three zig-zags that made little triangular peninsulas of skin project-ing from the side of the crevasse like stone platforms over an earthquake-shattered crust of earth. The bleeding had slowed to a trickle.

The scalp is a very vascular structure, the nurse was say-ing. Bleeds like stink, but because of that it doesn't often get infected. Still, we need to observe sterile technique. You need to reglove.

My lesson was under way.

This is a suture tray, she said, plopping a cloth-wrapped package onto the Mayo stand. I open the outer layer, you open the inner one. Be careful not to touch anything out-side the sterile field.

She peeled back the folded-napkin-like points of the sterile wrap.

Drape first, she said.

I draped. The wound lined up under the slit in the thick, heavily laundered cloth, the hems covering his forehead and eyes.

Well, you might let him see, she said. But don't contaminate your field.

Syringe, she said.

A glass monstrosity with brass rings sticking out from the barrel like Mickey Mouse ears, and the plunger that perfectly fit inside it, lay side by side. The ground-glass surfaces slipped together like fuzzy paper.

Xylocaine, 1 percent. She thrust the bottle in my face. You need to always double-check the label to be sure. It's routine.

I looked.

Well? she said.

Well, what? I said.

Say it.

Xylocaine, 1 percent, I repeated.

She squeegeed the rubber top with a cotton ball drenched in alcohol and pointed it to me. First draw 5 cc's of air.

I did that.

Now, with the larger needle, poke the top, push in the air, and draw out 5 cc's of solution.

It occurred to me that there was still a patient under all that wrapping we served over like a tablecloth. How are you doing, Sylvester? I asked.

You just do what you need to do, he said.

The nurse was peering over the wound. This will take about ten stitches — 2-0 silk. He'll probably take the full 5 cc's.

I must have looked as helpless as I felt.

Switch to the 25-gage needle — that's the smaller one — it doesn't hurt as much. And always inject *under* the edge of the wound into the tissue. Fewer nerve fibers there. Make little welts of Xylocaine all along the edges.

She went away.

I injected. Am I hurting you?

Sylvester laughed. Am I your guinea pig?

I guess so.

Just make it pretty, Doc.

I raised little mounds and waited. I tried to visualize how the edges, now somewhat swollen with fluid, trauma, and my little injections, would ever go back together. I imagined little buttons and loops and wondered if I would get it straight or manage in my bumbling to hook the button in the wrong buttonhole.

Use landmarks. The nurse was back, standing over my shoulder. Start at the ends and watch how the edges come together with each stitch.

She opened into the space of air above my table and let fall from there a curved needle with a black, thick, silk thread attached to the back end. Grasp it firmly in the hemostat and curl it in with your wrist, she said. She demonstrated the deep curvilinear motion that would gather the planes of tissue, pull them from the top and the base of the wound simultaneously to align them like a sealed fault line.

I decided to start at the jagged end because the parts seemed like interdigitating puzzle pieces. I looped a point into a trough.

You'll do fine, the nurse said. And disappeared.

I studied the wound. I visualized the pieces. I watched them come together several times before planting the suture needle, curving to its prescribed depth, matching that depth on the other side, then pushing the point through the volcano eruption of its own making on the other shore. I remembered the scene from the movie *Kidnapped* in which the pieces of the cup on the floor coming together was a visual trick used as a seduction into hypnosis. I snapped out of it and continued sewing.

I was three stitches in and feeling spunky. So how about this friend of yours? I asked.

What about him?

Sure it wasn't an enemy?

Don't have any of those.

Was he drunk?

Maybe so.

Have anything to do with a woman?

Maybe so.

Where did it happen?

The Cajun Bar.

Going back?

Soon as I get out of here.

How did the police find out about it?

They can smell blood a mile away.

Did you tell them anything?

Nothing.

Seems like they'd want to know who hit you.

They always want to know, but they don't expect to learn.

By this time I was beginning to notice a certain curvature to the far edge of the wound, the shape a bow makes when its string is drawn tight. My approximation of edges was imperfect. I pondered what to do.

I had six stitches in. I guessed I'd need three more. I decided to place them like spokes of a wheel whose imaginary center was where lines leaving the curve of the wound at right angles would intersect. My stitches, I decided, would follow those lines. That way the error would be equally distributed over each remaining stitch. Ol' Mattie Loventhal, my tenth-grade geometry teacher, would be proud.

Sylvester winced.

Sorry, I said. I guess I've taken so long the anesthesia's wearing off. I injected and started again.

And as I did so I felt a strong desire to know more about the life of the person who had become my patient, whose head I was injecting, whose blood and tissue fluid and shaved hair were on my hands.

Are you really sure you want to go back to the Cajun?

Yeah.

What about your, ah . . . friend?

Aww, he's done his thing. He'll be all right.

Seems to me the police should be taking care of him.

Sylvester laughed. You don't know nothing about that kind of life. It's live-and-let-live over there. The police don't interfere with us. We don't interfere with them.

But how does that work? As soon as I said it, I flushed with the feeling you get when you let your naive stupidity out of the box and you're just waiting there, hoping the other guy won't make you pay too bad.

He sighed. You don't want to know, Doc. You've got your world. They've got theirs. You don't want to know.

I finished the job and was surprised by the apparent absence of screwup.

Did you make it pretty, Doc?

Pretty pretty.

I guess that makes me your professor.

Sylvester stood, shucked the drapes like wrapping paper, and started buttoning his shirt.

You're worried, Doc. Don't be. The Cajun is all I got. It's all most people over there's got. And don't worry about my friend. I'll take care of him.

The resident popped in to glance at the handiwork, nodded and grunted, and started off for the door. He looked back over his shoulder and caught my eye. Come back next Friday night, Watts — he cast his thumb toward Sylvester — and you can sew up his friend.

I looked at Sylvester. Sylvester just walked out the door.

LOVE IS JUST A
FOUR-LETTER WORD

The wards of the General Hospital were large barns, patients lined up along the walls like cows in their stalls. Flimsy off-white curtains on rings conferred semipermeable privacy. The gaps, the absent rings, made it all relative.

Then, of course, sounds and smells knew no boundaries, bed to bed, stall to stall. They who were there shared one common experience. I saw a black-and-white photo once of the "old days." *Old*, old days at the General Hospital. There were no curtains then, but rather an all-pervasive light in the room and radiators lined up in the center aisle of the floor like involuntary radio transmitters in what must certainly have been a room overwhitened and overheated.

We rounded at eight o'clock. Every morning. Old patients got updates. New ones got complete clinical histories, presented by the intern on call during the previous night. I was the neophyte, the medical student who could not be expected to know much and whose blithered, half-opened eyes blinked from stall to stall, having already learned to expect the same old faces, old bodies, still there it seemed, past death.

That morning I saw in the distance, a distance usually approximating infinity between bed one and bed twelve, a young Latin woman whose drop-dead beauty was visible even from afar. Her presence made it difficult for me to concentrate on the updates of the old crones, wondering what disease she would have, and why such a spectacular jewel might be lying in our hospital.

Standing finally at the foot of her bed, the intern recited her history: third admission. All of them for gonorrhea septicemia.

I noticed the IV running. A piggyback infusion bag marked PCN dripped methodically.

Why septicemia? the resident asked.

She disseminates, the intern said. She spreads it everywhere in her body.

Why does she? asked the resident. The pelvis has a spectacular defense mechanism, evolved over centuries of survivalism. A girl just never knows what she'll come across in this world.

The resident paused for the expected sniggering, then went on, The pelvis protects against most anything.

Not pelvis, the intern said. Pharnyx.

It took a couple of beats to catch what was just said. Not pelvis.

I grew up in the South with its conservative behaviors,

lived in a "Christian" family, and all that—the girls I knew wouldn't let me touch them, much less give me a blow job.

The intern went on. She has some kind of localized susceptibility to this organism. The lymphatic system of her throat is selectively deficient. It allows the gonococcal organism, and only that organism, to slip past and gain access to the bloodstream. She doesn't disseminate from any other source or with any other infection.

But why three times?

She's monogamous. Same boyfriend each infection. The boyfriend refuses to get treated.

I felt like I was caught up in a freewheeling fiction.

The intern continued. She has the Snow White syndrome, he said.

Part of the job of the intern is to one-up everybody with facts or diagnostic pearls that no one else knows. It's a little game that keeps everyone on his toes. We suspected he'd made this one up.

Only in this case the poison apple was the boyfriend.

The resident was unimpressed. Seasoned. Less inclined to be moved by romantic eponyms. Why does she stay with him? he asked.

Or why does she keep going down on him? said the intern.

In that moment we became acutely aware of her, as if the questions we asked turned us that way. Everyone knew she had heard our discussion. Others in nearby beds, if they were conscious, would also have heard. Privacy was difficult, but could have been created by more discretion in what we said. There was something more to this extravagance of information at her expense. To be sure, most of the patients didn't care or wouldn't remember five minutes later. But we all knew she was different. Maybe we were just crude. Maybe we hoped this unflinching frankness, bringing her story out into the objective light of a medical teaching exercise, might give her a new perspective.

I was busy being in shock. First to be spellbound by her beauty and then stunned by the knowledge, entirely new to me, that a beautiful woman, knowing the consequences, would give herself so completely. It gave me goose bumps.

Ask *her,* the intern said.

We did.

She said nothing. Just turned her head to the pillow.

The resident stared at her with hard, knowing eyes. Love is just a four-letter word, he said, and moved on.

All day I watched her out of the corner of my eye. Her willingness, her vulnerability, made her beauty all the more striking. It was too much to bear.

Truth is, I could fall for her in a moment. She was the kind of woman who "needed protection." Someone who would keep her from harm. But I was a student, white coat and all that. Professional. We were in different worlds.

I went to her bedside. I said, You could die from this, you know.

Her round eyes misted. But she said nothing.

He should get treated. My words had no impact. Or arrested, I added with unexpected gusto.

She looked down at her hands.

I was overstepping, but I rationalized that it was out of concern for her, and pressed on. If he really loved you, I said, he would get the cure.

He *does,* she said. He *does* love me.

I realized this was the first time I had heard her voice. It was mellow, softer than I had imagined, but angry and insistent against the sharp sting of criticism.

You don't understand, she said. He just can't admit it's his fault.

Too much guilt?

No . . . he's . . . he's the kind of guy that believes nothing's ever wrong with him. So it's always my fault.

I felt rage for the creep, who, because of his own behavior, kept putting her life in danger. But I knew to say so would be futile. I thought I saw her sob gently. And suddenly I realized that if we were in the same world, I could love this woman.

Snap out of it, I told myself. And then asked her, So what are you going to do? You can't keep doing this.

The mist became a tear brimming the deep well of her eye. She rolled to the side, turning away from me and everything I stood for. She drew her hair back with two fingers, snuggled into the pillow, and closed her eyes, squeezing the reluctant tear into the space between us.

Close the curtain when you go, she said.

CIRCUS

Word sure do get around when the circus come to town, don't it, he said, referring to the crowds of nurses and interns come to see the cowboy who wouldn't take off his boots. Only when I sleep and make love, he said, and the hospital's no place for neither.

Vernon Dalton had a heart murmur. Fine by me, he said, five holes better than four any day. More love gets out. The problem was it gave him extra beats that bumped and rattled inside his chest. His heart flopped around like a bass in a bucket. His doctors sent him to the city to find out if it was dangerous.

In his hospital gown and boots, Vernon got hooked up to telemetry — heartbeat and misfire sent along radio waves to the nursing station down the hall, where the cardiac nurse watched for evidence of misfire.

We gave him IV Xylocaine to numb the errant heartbeat.

Problem is, it numbs part of the brain as well — makes some people go nuts.

Vernon was lying in his bed, minding his own business (which wasn't very much at the time), when one of his chest leads came unsnapped. Bells went off, lights flashed, and Vernon looked up to see a flat line on his monitor screen.

I'm dead, he said, and closed his eyes.

And he felt himself falling backward, space closing over him like water over stone. He felt something cool and attractive off to his left. His mother's voice seemed to be calling him there. But he seemed instead to be headed to that hot place off to his right.

Just then the nurse walked into the room and snapped the lead back on his chest. The alarm stopped. Heartbeats appeared on the screen. I'm alive, alive again, he said. I'm resurrected. I must be Jesus Christ!

Vernon stood up in the middle of his bed, boots and all, and began reciting scripture. He looked over at the wizened old lady in the bed beside him, pointed his finger at her, and said, *You* will be my first disciple.

The nurse shut off his Xylocaine.

It took a long time for Vernon to touch ground again. By then he had deputized eleven souls and delivered his Sermon on the Mount in the doctor's coffee room.

His heart condition was harmless and we sent him home. Last I heard, he'd become a right Christian young man who wanted to be sure he'd get to see his mother in heaven. He started appearing at revivals in those big tents, the ones with the out-of-tune pianos and the wide-vibrato gospel choirs, telling the multitudes that came to hear him about the time he died with his boots on and came back to life.

SURGICAL WOUND

Before he could even get to the bedside of his waiting patient, Dr. Bosky intercepted him, pulled him into a room for yet another of his little disciplinary lectures that were the only means of communication between the two doctors, once colleagues, now undeclared enemies passing unspeaking in the hall. Bosky was chief of the outpatient surgical unit, a position that, in the opinion of Dr. Heartfield, he had earned, but that gave too much power to his dark side, a power that had awakened what could only be described as a desire to discredit his competitors.

The patient, the lady with a little ganglion in her wrist, would need sedation in addition to local anesthesia. She was nervous — he knew that from what he had observed in the office. His attention had to be focused on her, ensuring that she was ushered through this little surgery with grace.

He walked alongside the gurney, opposite the nurse, Karen, who had witnessed the altercation but was silent. He had seen this silence before. Karen knew where her allegiances had to lie. She had a good job. She did what her chief said, even if it meant applying the rules of the unit unevenly.

He could feel her silence. He was in no mood to involve her at any level with this conflict. Her sympathies were predictable.

He spoke in even tones to his patient. This is simple, he said. I've never lost anyone during this surgery and I don't intend to do so today.

I needed to hear that, she said. But I still want drugs.

Drugs you get. Kickapoo Joy Juice, if you want. We're going to make you comfortable.

And how are you today, Doctor? she asked.

Fine. The doctor had paused a beat before answering. Now he rushed through the rest. I'm just fine.

Karen was applying the EKG leads, speaking softly to the patient, informing her what she was doing and what to expect next. He chose not to look at Karen, not needing to field whatever aggravation might surface there.

I'm going to make a little incision and just pop that thing out. It's very simple. And I'll sew you up real purdy-like.

The patient laughed. Karen smiled a little and went on with her work.

He knew he had not worked through the altercation in his mind or his heart. Both were necessary, but they would have to wait. He would set it aside like an unanswered page from the answering service.

The wrist was in position, operative light in place, surgical set open aseptically on the Mayo stand. He was gowned and gloved and masked for action.

I like to use a little Versed and Demerol, he said. The Versed is a quick-acting Valium, the Demerol a light narcotic. Together they'll make you silly.

And make your work easier, she said.

And make my work easier.

He felt himself moving through the scene as if he were watching from the outside, a reader of an Edgar Allan Poe short story in which he knew the circumstance but maintained the reader's distance. Even the figures in the drama moved with deliberate grace, as if in a long literary sentence in which every detail sparkled with clarity.

The patient was drifting now. He knew he would not be required to entertain or reassure her much longer. He would only have to walk with her a short distance more in the lighted hallway of consciousness and then a solitude would come in which reflection could return. He wasn't sure he wanted reflection. The event of the morning trembled inside him even while his attention was fully elsewhere.

He began the surgery. Karen was at his side, anticipating. He didn't like her political stance, but he had to admit he admired her professionalism. They rarely exchanged compliments, or glances, like those congressmen across the aisle from one another who don't feel compelled to call attention to the virtues of their political rivals. Still, she admired him, he could tell. Both for his smooth, careful way with patients and for his surgical technique. More than once she had said,

You make it look easy. I wish the residents could see you work.

Another sore point. Bosky had all the residents. By stealth he had squeezed out his competitors. There was no talking to the man. It was clear that it was best to simply show up, shut up, and scoot home with the minimum of interaction. Fewer heart attacks that way.

Funny how reflection surfaced now and not while he was coaxing his patient into a sense of confident relaxation, as if reflection and attending to the patient occupied the same space, but now, while performing a simple but delicate surgery in which highly focused concentration was required, he could feel the rush of—what was it?—anger? frustration? Maybe it was that cancerous mass of emotion that sprang from the sense of not feeling valued.

Karen was attentive, quiet.

I think she could use a little more Versed, he said to her.

Karen reached over his arm for the three-way stopcock that housed the tip of the loaded syringe attached by its tubing directly to the patient's brain. It lay on the bed-sheets a little way from her. Instead of walking around, or pulling the IV tubing to draw it near, she leaned gently into his arm as she reached over him to open the stopcock and slowly push in 1 cc of velvety fluid.

He was aware of her pressing against him, of the soft beginnings of her breasts under her gown as at first they grazed his upper arm, then pressed confidently to him. He felt no need to withdraw, or to ease her access to the Versed.

She felt no need to alter the arrangement by which he now had come to feel strangely warmed, this proximity of femaleness, this softness into which he could fall into the lover, the mother, into forgiveness in all its unspoken terms.

She said nothing, as nothing was expected. Both looked only to their tasks. Outwardly she could have no safe way to offer her sympathies, if she had any. Yet the body could speak in ways untraceable and immeasurable. She was taking a long time to push in the Versed. Time slowed and did not want to speed. No one was impatient or anxious.

There was just an open wound and a confident sense in the room that all would be well again.

TELEPHONE TREE

Mary Casey needs her Zyrtec refilled. She's having an allergic reaction and she's out of pills.

Her chart appears on my desk, and because she's in an HMO, there's a Post-it attached with an 800 number written on it.

I dial the number. A message says I have reached the National/International Consolidated Prescription Service Center and the call may be randomly monitored to ensure quality. I know what I'm in for, and here it is. I am given four options:

If I am calling about myself or a family member, press 1.

If I am a doctor's office, hospital, or pharmacy, press 2.

If I am calling from an area outside my home telephone area code, press 3.

If I want all this in Spanish, press 4.

Here we go, I say, and press 2.
More options.

To access the automated member eligibility information
    line, press 1. [Is that an automated eligibility or an
    automated member?]
If you are seeking medication or prescription authoriza-
    tion, or have benefit inquiries, press 2. [Didn't we do
    this already?]
For questions about claims, press 3.
For credentialing, capitation, or to speak with a
    provider-relations representative, press 4.
For all other inquiries, press 5.

Just for fun I thought I'd press 7, but I hated like hell to
have to start all over again.
I press 2. More options.

If you are calling about benefits or eligibility, press 1.
If you are calling about prescription information, press
    2. [Is there an echo in here?]
For all other inquiries, press 3.

I consider the possibility that there is a plot afoot to
make doctors all over the country press 2 a certain number
of times in order to induce mass hypnosis. I break the
rhythm. I use a different finger, the middle one, and
press 2 . . . again.

If you are calling about a refill too soon or a vacation
   override, press 1. [What the hell is a vacation override? I imagined a vacation gone mad, snarfing up all
   the remaining dates on the calendar, then the next
   year's calendar, then the millennium . . .]
For all other pharmacy questions, press 2.

Just call me a sheep on Soma. 2 it is.

There's a break and a voice comes on the line. At last! I
exclaim, a REAL PERSON!

Silence at the other end. It's dead over there. No sense
of humor. Maybe I was a bit hasty about that real-person
business.

Is this about a prescription refill? she asks.

I imagine an automaton on the other end of the line. I
could point out that I've pressed that option four times
already and that if she just looked at her computer she
would know the answer to that question, but I'm staying
cautious. Yes, I say. It's Mary Casey's Zyrtec.

Do you have her member number?

Damn! Got me already, I say. Check and mate.

Silence again.

What was her name?

C-a-s-e-y.

First name?

M-a-r-y.

Do you have her date of birth?

I thumb through the chart thinking about palm trees on

a desert island, windsurfing sails, the beach filled with 10s from the agencies of Beverly Hills . . . Twelve/twenty-nine/fifty-five, I say.

Who are you?

Marley's Ghost! I'm Doctor Watts. W-a-t-t-s, David.

Telephone number?

I give it.

License number?

I give it.

Narcotics Prescription Number?

I give it.

What prescription did you want?

Zyrtec, ZYRTEC, ZYRTEC — I can hear my voice rising in front of the scream shackled at the back of my throat. That's Z-y-r-

She cuts me off. Have you tried Claritin?

Christ! Who's the doctor here! I am just about to lose it. But I know what she's doing. This is one of those questions designed to piss you off so much that you throw the phone against the wall and break the connection. Then the National/International Center for Discontent, or whatever it is, doesn't have to pay for the prescription.

I can't remember, I say. Maybe we have, maybe not. Anyway, Zyrtec works best for her. That's why I'm refilling it.

She was, she says.

Was what?

Was tried on Claritin. I see it here.

There is not a civilized phrase in the universe I have left

to say. Now I understand why the phone conversation is being recorded.

When did this patient first come to see you? she asks.

A soft humming noise is becoming audible at the periphery of my brain. I discover it in the back of my throat, a sound like the sound on the leading edge of the roar of a samurai warrior just before charging headlong into his opponent. But . . . I am determined . . . to get Mary . . . her prescription. I shuffle through the chart. Four—mmm—twelve—yeah—ninety-eight, I say with undisguised satisfaction. YES!

What's her diagnosis?

Jeez, next you'll want my mother's library card!

Not a glimmer at the other end of the line. Not a beat. I am dealing with a hardened professional.

Her throat swells up and she can't breathe, I say. Ruins her day. Angioneurotic edema, if you want a term for it.

Silence again.

I figure if silence works for her, it can work for me. Seconds pass. If I had been talking to Jerry Davalos down at Ace Pharmacy, this whole transaction would have taken fifteen seconds. Is it possible to become so conditioned to this kind of harassment you accept it as standard procedure? God forbid. Silence still. I can feel the quiet pressure of my patients waiting in the outer office. They must be wondering what's going on. But I will not relent. I let the silence run . . . and run . . . and run . . .

Five minutes, and she's back.

I'll approve it for six months, she says. Then quickly adds,
as if not to admit defeat, But not a minute longer.

I have many choices what to say here. The day has been
long. My patients are waiting.

Thanks, I say . . . and hang up the phone.

STRICTURE

I press my finger in the channel until resistance grows too great. His brow is raised, his eyes closed, his chin lifted as in prayer. The stricture is first muscular, thick and slow, like clay hardening in the wall of a quarry. I lean in with my whole body and press for the membrane I know is up there. I can tell when I get to it. It will be sharp on the tip of my finger, like the scrape of an iron ring.

He is sedated—his request and mine. We've been here before and we both know what we're up against. Even after large amounts of Demerol, Versed, *and* droperidol, he quakes against this invasion as if to shake a bad dream.

I speak in tones low and calm, as if to compose a startled horse, spooked and taut at the edge of flight: *Easy now, just a little more pressure. Okay, I've stopped. Let's take a little rest and then we'll go on.* My job is to reach the membrane. And break it open.

Much will be forgotten and much muted by the cloak of

chemistry I throw over him. Even so, pain rises from his body like vapor, and reluctance swells within me like that cinch that froze my hand once in its arc of anger over my child. I remember that hand, having begun its descent to spank, halted, not by intent but by some unknown force, as if the body in its wisdom had the will to interfere with itself, refusing to carry out the errant command. Where are the nerve fibers for that antipathy to violence, I wondered. I don't know. But it was clear that even a deluge of rage could not wash them away.

Now, I shudder against that same resistance, but I hold my place. I have learned that he will not be helped if I shy from my task. I disregard his pleas. I have learned how to do this.

Now the time for the push. I call forth the savage beast that, like the cat, unresponsive to the squeals of the dying mouse in its paws, feels nothing. It sweeps through my body with a shudder. My face contorts, my breath gathers for the scream that will not scream, and together we put aside aversion to pain, antipathy to violence, the protective mechanisms that keep us humane, a paresis just long enough to let me finish: to let me feel the membrane scrape and tear.

I withdraw.

We rest and return to ourselves.

We have been flogging the aftermath of Crohn's disease, which, by its festering, has turned his rectum into a tar pit of infection and seepage. By all accounts he should have had surgery long ago, a bypass to divert the fecal stream and allow this soppy bog a chance to heal. He has refused.

He shows no signs of disease. He is handsome. He is young. He smiles a lot. He wants to keep it that way. No ostomies, he says. No surgery.

The future has so many arms. How can I tell where we will be even a few minutes from now? I do not know, for example, that months later I will refer him to a major inflammatory bowel center and he will not return, not schedule another of these sessions. All this moment knows is that the stricture is open, report typed, documentation attached, and copies sent to doctors who need to hear about it. He is sleeping, drifting in that rare caesura of peace that blesses gently before he rises again, stretches, goes back to work, and signs up to play softball with his colleagues this weekend, they who think they know him but have no idea what he's going through, no notion that the two of us are cruising toward the next time, when we meet like reluctant warriors and do it all again.

ATTRACTION

The intern was shocked by her beauty. She moved effortlessly among her patients, like a breeze in the olive trees at sunset.

He was there to make rounds on the Guillain-Barré patient, a young man with that mysterious neurological disease that paralyzes slowly, ascending the spine like snake toxin: first legs, then arms, and then . . . you can't take a breath.

The respirator did that for him, attached by a flexible tube to his tracheostomy, a hole in his neck that let the air move more easily in and out. Stable. No problems. It would only be a matter of time until the paralysis released its hold and he would be well again, able to return to a normal life.

She was his nurse, bending over him now to remove the little bits of mucus that collected like raindrops in his tube, detaching him from his respirator for a few seconds as she gently suctioned him. He was awake, not able to talk, not able to move. He could only blink his eyelids to show appreciation or fear.

Her long black hair brushed against his shoulders and arms as she moved over him. The intern watched, imagining her hair touching *his* arms, *his* face. She took no notice of him, but he thought he could feel a surge of energy from her, as in that moment when the air in the room ripples toward you, as if she says, in that way, I am opening toward you.

He would introduce himself later. He made a little vow as he left the makeshift ICU — those thrown-together collections of the more seriously ill in the days before automatic monitoring equipment with alarms to warn people of decreasing oxygen, fading blood pressure, a unit entirely dependent upon the close scrutiny of the staff — left to write his note in the chart, wondering if he had a chance with her.

When he finished, he returned to the bedside. He was accustomed to seeing the patient lying still, but there was something different about him now, something strange, as if he were stiller than still. Then it hit him. There was no sign of life. The pulse was gone. Pupils were dilated and fixed. No motion anywhere, just the bobbing of respirator tubing, detached and wavering three inches above his tracheostomy, pushing its noise over the wide expanse of his eyes.

The nursing supervisor came, reconnected the tubing, whisked away the nurse, and began the necessary conversations with the relatives outside the ICU door. It was a terrible disease, they might say, to take the very young. So unpredictable that way.

But the intern could replay the details: the little ritual of suction, the patient watching, blinking his eyes, a little sign of distraction on the face of the nurse, the urge to say, Warning, warning, oh no, be careful, rising like a fist of wind inside him, then the quick blinking, the flutter of eyelids to interrupt what it knew it could not interrupt, waiting for the detached respirator to be noticed, to be attached, as the lights in the room began to fade around the walls where they met with the edge of his vision, the tight cinch against movement or speech unyielding *even for this* as the tubing hovered, within reach . . . out of reach, no one responding . . . to his quiet petition. Consciousness . . . fading, still conscious of his fate . . . conscious . . . of . . . until the blinking . . . stopped.

Monologue Millie and the System of Care

Millicent calls to say she has fired her caseworker. She's always firing her caseworker. Then hiring her back. Reconciliations like these that repeat themselves are littered with scars and driftwood, and assume, increasingly, an air of impermanence. A mood that, incidentally, matches her world if she were to think about it; more impermanent than her persistence on my telephone would suggest, having survived colitis, a hip fracture, a psychotic son, and multiple nursing homes where the care was, in her words, reprehensible, survived all that to dial me up seven times so far this day.

I remind her that in order to take adequate care of the cellulitis on her leg, she either needs to be in the hospital or to accept the visiting nurses I send her. She prefers instead to call, to instill in my secretary a sense of dire urgency that could overwhelm even the best protectorate, secure a wedge of time in a daily schedule already apprehended by the need and demand of patients more willing to play by the rules than she is, and then show up five hours late, just before the office closes, to undo her legs in my waiting room.

The scene is dramatic. Ceremonious. And very effective. My other patients waiting there are drawn to deep empathetic explosions of support, and I feel—though at the same time I realize I could be making this up—that this performance swings the pointer of anonymous inquisition directly at me. For example, how could I let one of my patients be so humiliated?

She's not humiliated. But I do not explain this to the audience, nor do I justify. I bend over her with the gesture of a country doctor attending gangrene at the roadside and release what tensions I may have into the beatitudes of care. It is a play with a plot and a protagonist (in my version, myself) who, helpless in the face of providence, gives in to the power of appearances. Classic stuff. None will know she is *unregulatable*. She will come see me when she wants to. Exactly.

I return from a few days away to find she is in the hospital. No one seems to know how she got there, only that she has called three times this morning complaining that the house staff wants to discharge her. Prematurely, of course. I take the elevator to the twelfth floor. She is on the phone when I go into her room. He eyes are closed and she is speaking through a fixed smile.

Good morning, Pier 39. I have news for you. Yesterday was Saturday and Sunday. Today is Halloween.

You see, I persuaded them to remove the twenty-ninth and there wasn't any thirtieth. You may think this is Monday the thirtieth, but it's really the thirty-first. I made them give me the twenty-ninth to keep as a souvenir. Oh, Doctor Watts, you're here. Good.

Well, the last time I was here I begged to leave. But it was the day before the weekend and I couldn't go. They suffered a little calendar confusion then as well.

But I hope they come to get this bedpan. I have signaled them.

My home is not ready for me. They have insinuated that I have not been taking care of myself. There were a couple of glitches with medications, I confess. And I thought it best when Monique got so heavy-handed, bursting in, pushing me around—I asked her to leave my house. I've never been so angry in my life.

But this big production led to my arrival in an ambulance. There was my caregiver standing in the door with this *expression* on her face. There I was with my legs that needed taking care of. So I apologized to her. I do what I can. And I myself got a new refrigerator. Got a new toilet, but there are some problems. It is small, shaped like an egg. Does not fit my buttocks.

At this point, not seeing any clearing in the weather report, and realizing I couldn't wait long for such an opening,

I began the routines I usually do in such circumstances, only not accompanied by the usual commentary, as, in this case, it would be uphill and, anyway, probably without much in the way of recognition.

So, by this time I have examined her legs, not interrupting, but signaling with my hands what I was intending to do. She, responding with a nod or a gesture of the hand, arranges herself while she keeps on talking.

But it was so horrible where I lived after the fire in Pacific Heights. I couldn't afford it. I had a hard time, so I sat on the brick wall between the two backyards. It was a heritage building. It was built by a father who had two daughters in the same wedding.

I can perhaps survive, but I can't walk. They say I can. The first day they said, Oh no, don't get up, so I stayed in the bed three days. Now I can't walk at all.

I'm now working on getting the old toilet seat back. It's an old Kohler toilet. And smaller than an egg. I'm trying to get grab bars. But I'm not going to install them. This is an old building and you never know what you are going to get into.

And I thought, Can I really live in this building? But I said to myself, I have to get out of that horrible building next to Macy's with the fire upstairs. Came back from volunteering at the General Hospital. Fire upstairs. Took me half an hour to determine I had no fire. I had a flood — that's what I came out of.

The cellulitis is improved, I have determined by my little

examination conducted in parallel—the kind of progress that comes from simple interventions applied simply: heat, elevation, and your basic intravenous antibiotics. I am pleased. She continues her story.

Well, I managed to find I had this toilet problem. I wanted to invite Monique back home. I wanted to do everything I could to make it safe.

Let me tell you the Nurses Plus story. I was discharged early. In this situation I had a very excellent man. He knew we needed a special dressing. He came back. But he didn't pay much attention to my request to have him call your office. (But before 11:30.) He disappeared on the other side of the room—I cannot see across the bed in the arrangement that's been made. I cannot recall the name of the orthopedist who suggested that we use a love seat with a pillow at the head and to elevate the feet. Hospitals don't want you to do that. But it's very effective.

I had even arranged to sleep on a futon like the Japanese do, but I feel that would bother everyone.

But I'm telling you I really have picked my way through a minefield. And I have to say that I was more amused than annoyed by this calendar episode. I do know the date. And I have been established as competent.

I murmur something, reach for the blood-pressure cuff, and begin unobtrusively wrapping it around her arm.

Why are we keeping people around who really don't want to be here? I've seen people at Laguna Honda who pray to be taken before morning. I don't see myself there—

I have no great pain at the moment. I don't exactly have a son and I'd really like to have one to discuss this with. The household was the household. We must accept it as it is. We need to forgive each other. But I can't.

I release the cuff. Her pressure is higher than usual. I don't report it and decide to chalk it up to the subject matter.

It was almost unendurable, my sister's death. They were talking only to my son. The *heir*. He was insisting on the operation, but I had the durable power. I knew what was going on between my sister and my son. They meant much to each other, but they would not let me see her record. My son read it every morning. It was a little difficult.

But the doctors were kindly. They let me hole up in Bronson Institute, said I'd be perfectly safe so long as I kept the door shut.

I have learned to schedule my visits with Millie when there is a terminus, in this case my patient with rectal bleeding eleven floors down on the endoscopy suite table, waiting for me. Lost, but recorded somewhere, is the assertion I made when I first entered the room that I had only a short time to be here. I call it forth now. She says fine, fine. But as I quicken my steps to the elevator I can hear her conversation still going like the horn of a diesel locomotive already passed, softening down the tracks in the distance. I will come back later. Or . . . not.

As I wonder what will come next I reflect that she is too eloquent to be declared insane, too insane to be responsible, and too easily offended to adhere to a constant path.

The next day I am in the middle of an endoscopy when Rich passes me a note. The way he does this is to crack the door, reach around the facing like an anonymous hand snatching a coin — only in reverse — and stick this Post-it to the door facing. It says MB on the twelfth floor has called. Her number is busy, so I walk up to see her.

She is on the phone. Sees me and tells whoever it is she has to go.

They are struggling with me, I know that. I didn't intend to call you at the endoscopy unit, but your secretary insisted and Rich was very nice and said that it would be okay. They've been working on my constipation.

Additionally, I think I'm bothersome by not taking all the medications all together as they wish me to. I like to space them out, but I try not to make too many difficulties. But they're not sure if I will take over. I sympathize with that.

I'm not trying to make a problem, I just would like to go home. It's not UC, it's the payment system. We know that. It's a serious time. We should do better.

And I'm trying not to get taken over in conservatorship. Because then I would be useless. So I've been talking to the State of California and have found a sensitive person in the Department of Health. I've lost all my file cards. But I have his name somewhere . . . so it's . . . everywhere . . . nowhere . . . here somewhere.

Oh, my!

Yesterday they were going to get security and shove me in the vehicle. But now they seem to be doing it by the book. The first time they forced me home, they sent people in. They were making the bed up under me. It was a wild scene. But I put up with it.

I haven't got my calcium today, but some of the nurses have been wonderful. One has not. I like Russians. I even speak a little. Every time she enters the room she takes the curtain and throws it back. I could be sitting on the commode — whatever. So I reported her and she has, since that time, been difficult.

I, adhering to my plan, have already started examining her legs.

Because of the Raynaud's I need an extra wrap. But yesterday I was uncovered to my knees for the longest time. It was the one on this leg — they removed the dressing. Finally I put socks on it myself. Eventually I did get the nurses and we are trying to find a robe to cover my shoulders and we haven't achieved that. But that's okay.

It was Bill. No, that's not quite right, it starts with an *H*. Okay. Well. He's a very good physical therapist. He could see, contrary to the story "Well, you're doing fine," that not all was well. Because of the Lasix I was getting floods of water. So I got out of bed. But they stopped me. They put the walker in front of me. I had a terrible time taking a shower and my head was wet so I took this cantilevered light over the bed like this up against my neck to dry out my hair. That's why we need advocates.

You asked me would I go to Laguna Honda Hospital and I sure would. They don't like me there. They know me: Millicent Barker, UC disaster. But I was there to help the lady with her leg cut off. The problem with the Mariposa is they order you around like cops. And the rooms are depressing unless you decorated them yourself. And the food was excellent, but I know that it is often excellent on the day you are there.

And, of course, my property has gone *whhppffiitttttt* with all this going on.

When you're in a wheelchair and you go to any desk like Neurology, that desk is so high you're only seeing their nose, if that. I'd like to see that changed. Well, I was in a wheelchair and I had gone into the disabled bathroom — you couldn't use it. So I called to have it fixed.

And while she was speaking I confirmed to my satisfaction that the evidence of cellulitis was indeed gone. It was safe for her to go home. Well, as safe as it would ever be.

We're trying to quiet the wards. You can wear earphones. We've changed M-15. You know M-15. Oh yes. I know. It's the admitting ward. Yes. It is transformed. It is as quiet as can be. And the voices of the nurses are different.

I raised my hand.

I know. You have to go. I just wanted to let you know how I'm trying to help out and bring you up to date. They say I'm diabetic. Have been since I hit the hospital. That's news to me. I wish they'd tell me. But I assume you know that. I'd like to stay until tomorrow evening.

Will you go and talk to her? To Doctor Silverstone? She wasn't so nice on rounds this morning. She's usually nice. She's beginning to push. A little shovel action, I guess.

I turn to the door, placing her request among those that get filled if the occasion to fill it comes along. It must be tough to be so concerned about issues of so little concern to most of us, even those who are in the business of care. I wonder how she persists in what seems to be an intensive, dedicated concern. Is she never lonely?

I go to her chart. I want to see how the house staff is holding up. And I want to know about the diabetes thing, the subject of substance that finally surfaces after hours of fluff. And I read:

> *Pt. eval yest. Rec short term SNF placement or d/c*
> *home c 24 hr home health & PT.*
> *afebrile. taking dicloxacillin qid*
> *S. feels not ready to leave hospital as "I need more*
> *Physical Therapy"*
> *c/o lump in throat. unsure if improves drinking fluid*
> *feels legs look better*
>
> *O. VA Tm 37 65-75 135-165/65-75 20 97% RA*
> *I/O good po*
> *Exam Gen 82 yo lying in bed awake . . .*
>
> *. . . medically remains stable for d/c Pt aware. Have*
> *arranged house PT. will discuss d/c w/SW*
> *[unintelligible], MS4*

Nothing about diabetes.

Next day I call her room around noon.

Oh, Doctor Watts, I've been trying to get ahold of you. I am thinking that the solution they have proposed is not the right one for me. Because it is a Somatocor organization. As you know, Somatocor has no use for Mrs. MB. Therefore, if I am a UC disaster . . . I don't know. I don't know what to do for the body.

If you think it's the best thing to do, I will do it. I thought you were in my camp and I want to go on thinking it. But there are people who are confusing and appear to want to be. And now I am told I am hostile, I am passive-aggressive. I suppose that is their last thing to throw at me. I don't think that should happen.

The problem is the friendlies from Washington — and is there any way this can be used as an example? — I don't think they want to hurt people. Of course we've got Bush now, don't we. Yes. So there you are.

This is not to my best liking, but I am told to be thankful and appreciative and gracious. And I will try to do so.

We hang up. I am struck by the fact that in spite of her having finally consented to my request for her to go to the Step-Down Unit for extended care, I really have very little to do with how things have turned out. Instead of my usual role, in which opinions are listened to and often followed, in this case I am more like a stopover, a nesting box for geese in migration. Maybe it is not my role to alter the impact of disease after all; maybe I can only introduce a little sway in the hammer's arc.

Halfway down the hall my cell phone is ringing again. My receptionist will need psychotherapy when I get there. I will ask her to spend time on a project where there is some hope of a positive return. Require her to use her judgment. She will need to apply the graceful art of hanging up without offense. Learn to recognize, as best she can, the event or the trend of events that might be dangerous. Leave the rest to me. And to fate. It is all we can do. My receptionist is troubled. Maybe I will bring her flowers.

Maybe some for Millicent, too.

PART

TWO

Waiting to Be Served

The man with the beard, wearing tennis shoes, a ski hat, and a sleeveless red vest, escorts his friend to the car.

The friend is stiff. He waddles and ooches in a way that I, having had various appendages of my own temporarily disabled, can understand.

The man opens the door for his friend. His friend falls in. The car on cue bows in response. A cup of coffee in a Styrofoam container sits on the roof. In the moment that passes between equilibrium in the passenger seat and the instant the man reaches for the cup and hands it to his friend, there is, for the man, a little breath, in and out, and for his friend, anticipation, waiting to be served.

I know about this. My mother, though she lived to be ninety, was always sick or on the verge of something or other. She created within this inhospitable geography of illness a realm of comfort by always recruiting little moments of service like these: my father, in the kitchen scrambling eggs, her boys bringing wildflowers to the bedside, everyone tiptoeing through the rooms in what came to be a ghostlike passage of childhood. We didn't like giving service, but we got to be very good at it.

I've even wondered if that's part of the reason I became a doctor, and why, though committed to service, I resist behaviors that service generates. Be strong. Recover. Resist the idea of pain . . . the disease and the disease it makes.

And it doesn't make me tough on my patients. On the contrary, it gives me a basis for understanding where they are, and, out of that, more tolerance.

Mavis calls, complaining of constipation. It's seven thirty in the morning. The urgency is that she's deathly afraid to fly and she's booked on tomorrow's plane to Hawaii with her husband. She wants me to tell her she can't go. Well, I have layers of response to that, all the way from "It's all right if you don't go" to "Just do what you have to do and stop whining about it." Well, I guess I wouldn't say that. I'm too well trained.

I know, I know, there's a fuzzy sense of well-being that rises from attention received. It lights up faces. It's an expression of affection, after all. And it does wonders. And I love doing it, but it's tricky. The circumstance is born out of need, and need . . . well, need can always be questioned. So the server either has to commit to the legitimacy of the request or wonder if he's being manipulated. It's natural to doubt, to try to protect yourself a little. Yet when either the disease or the diseased is convincing, doubt, and all the self-protection it provides, is crushed.

So the friend receives his coffee, but he is made to wait just a little. Mavis will be funneled into a pathway that takes her to the airport, but the ceremony will contain a few grumbles.

The man is walking around his car. He is unlocking the door.

I don't know him.

I know him very well.

Flu Shot

She stood in my examining room unable to sit, pacing, then stopping tensely, as if paralyzed by the urge to pace. Three times she had made this appointment, three times a no-show. My secretary raised her eyebrow when she came in. But I had nothing to say.

Now her eyes touched and glided, touched and glided over me like the scan of an electron microscope, programmed for the penetrating search.

I fetched the vaccine, rended the silver packet for its sterile pledget, swabbed the red nipple of the rubber disk at the top, then plunged and withdrew just the right 0.5 cc amount. I had anticipated this visit.

I asked if she was ready. She said yes. And now the killed virus I injected into the dense fibrils of her shoulder would evoke from the rangy lymphocytes their molecules of protection. She winced, turned to go, then turned back.

Why did he have to die? And as she says this her body gives a little seizurelike lurch. Couldn't you have prevented it?

I was gathering the detritus I had left behind: the silver crimps of packet walls torn open, the needle guard, the soiled pledget with its spot of blood in the center, the dangerous needle I would place in the red plastic carton marked Hazardous. I remember his last office exam, sixty-two years old. Healthy. We focused on a few small problems with his cholesterol medications. As a part of his general workup I might have ordered a sigmoidoscopy. I did not. In my ear I could hear the admonitions of hospital lawyers cautioning me not to say too much. Don't commit yourself, they might say. And I felt—what was it?—something like the shame of being caught doing something wrong. But in the cavity of that humiliation, finally exposed, I felt no desire to waffle or dodge. She deserved better than that.

Yes, I said. The cancer might have been prevented. And then there was just me and her and the truth in the room.

Strange, she said. All those years with you and with the doctor before you, nobody ever recommended a sigmoidoscopy. If that had been done the year before, would you have caught the cancer in time?

The detritus was removed. The needle was in its safe place. I had no urge to fidget in the face of her question.

It's possible, I said, if it were still a polyp. Or if it hadn't spread too far. And I realized that though this was true, it was a manner of deflection. I was drawn to return to the unadorned answer. It's possible, I said. It's possible it could have been prevented.

She was silent.

I was silent.

She waited, then . . .

I have no one. No children, no family. He was all I had.

I nodded.

She reached for her overcoat.

You'll probably have to do something about this or let it go, I said. All this hurt will come to no good.

I would never do anything, she said. I like you. I think you are a good doctor. I want — I think I want — to continue to come and see you — but it will be hard.

I'm sorry, I said. And I want you to know that I believe you should do what you need to do even if it means . . .

No, no. Well, maybe. I don't know.

She left. And returned for her flu shot the following year, and the year after, never mentioning her husband, and then, eventually, for her own screening sigmoidoscopy, well in advance of its time, a request I filled as an obedient pharmacist might fill an unusual prescription, knowing it was too early, but conscious of the fear she was facing, conscious of the forgiveness she brought, coming to me for the help I might give, the test that might have saved her husband.

THE MORBIUS MONSTER

Billy Claymeyer had indigestion. For as long as he could remember, he had a burning sensation in his chest and throat, usually after eating. For years he had put off going to see a doctor, but the symptoms worsened, and he thought, still with some reluctance, it might be time.

I advised the usual therapies: antacids, H2 blockers, elimination of coffee, chocolate, and alcohol from the diet—nothing worked. Because of the long duration of symptoms and the possibility he might by now have a more aggressive form of esophagitis called Barrett's esophagus, a condition in which the cells of the lining begin a precancerous transformation, I recommended endoscopy.

The idea of endoscopy is scary—a snakelike tube with a light for a mouth, pushed down your throat—but with a little information most people recognize that the fear is worse than the event itself, and generally the motivation to be free of annoying symptoms, or to avert danger, overcomes resistance. The reality is, it only lasts five minutes, and the patients are pleasantly sedated so they don't experience discomfort. Considering what's happening, it all goes remarkably well.

But Billy refused.

Patients know their bodies. They have a sixth sense I have learned to respect. So I am accustomed, without much dissent, to endorsing their wishes as long as they are not clearly harmful. In this case there seemed to be no urgency. That, combined with a look on his face I could only describe as untamed dread, made me let it slide.

Billy was about thirty-five, a somewhat inward man with a tendency not to volunteer his thoughts or feelings. He was an accountant with a large number of clients who delighted in his intelligence and regard for duty. It seemed to me that his decision not to do endoscopy was inconsistent with his exacting manner in business. I concluded it must be for reasons not apparent on the surface.

I prescribed a stronger antacid, advised him again regarding diet and activity, and asked him to return in one month.

He returned admitting the symptoms were no better and that he had started waking up at night with pain. It sounded like he was now having symptoms of ulcer disease in addition to those he already had of reflux esophagitis. Diagnostic categories blurred. Choice of therapy would be impacted. Outcomes would become less predictable. I brought up endoscopy again. After long consideration, he agreed.

He arrived at the endoscopy suite asking to be put all the

way out. I don't want to know anything about it, he said. I reassured him I would make him comfortable and gave the usual doses of Demerol and Versed. He appeared to be adequately sedated, but as I touched him to begin the procedure, he pushed me away. I gave more medications. Same problem. He rose from deep sleep to perform this act of rejection again and again. I increased the sedation. But the more I sedated him, the worse it got.

I was in a range of dosing that is unusual except for patients with a history of alcohol abuse or long exposure to tranquilizers or sedatives. Billy had neither, yet his resistance to sedation was phenomenal.

We were bordering on deep sedation, where the respiratory center in the brain becomes suppressed and proper oxygen levels are hard to maintain without external assistance. We could sedate no further. Yet still he rose up against the endoscope. I spoke to him through the haze, reminding him it would take only a few minutes, would not hurt, and if we couldn't get it done this time, we would have to cancel the test.

It was difficult. He moaned, almost cried, as we guided the scope along its path. Several times he reached up to pull it out, and we had to start over. Against all that sedation he was still able to fight and resist. I hurried and finished the exam in two minutes. The findings were interesting and worth the effort, for in addition to reflux esophagitis he had a gastric ulcer. The biopsy returned three days later showing *Helicobacter pylori,* the ulcer-causing bacteria.

In the office I gave him the report, switched his medications, and added antibiotics. I told him he was likely to do much better now.

Then I asked about his experience with endoscopy.

He remembered nothing.

You put up quite a struggle, I said.

That's what the nurses said. Sorry.

Oh no. No need to apologize. I'm just concerned about whatever it was that made you fight so hard against a procedure that is basically simple and safe. Do you have any thoughts?

No idea, he said.

I had reflected back on my interactions with Billy, looking for any clues we might explore. I knew we would need endoscopy again to tell us if the ulcer had healed, and I wanted to protect him from another dreadful experience, even if he didn't remember it afterward.

I was struck by the fact that the experience never made it into his consciousness. Amnesia is common after endoscopy, but one would expect that after such a violent, willful opposition there would be some shadow of awareness. The psychic strength needed to erase that force from memory would have to be huge.

Is there anything in your past experience that might have a bearing on this?

Not that I know of.

He shifted uncomfortably in his chair. Something moved uneasily behind the screen of his face.

I decided to use another patient as an example. I thought it might take some of the pressure off.

You know, I had another patient who had a difficult time. I thought it might be emotional, since if you think about it in the cool of the day as we are now, there's no reason for that magnitude of fear.

I watched his eyes, conscious that I might be teasing a demon. I saw only interest. A little curiosity, perhaps. I pressed on.

The endoscope is a rather phallic object, I said, still watching his eyes.

He nodded.

In my other patient's case I guessed she might have had a past experience, perhaps abuse as a child, her subconscious still smarting—no, terrorized is a better word—by the memory. Sedation numbs the rational mind, and with it the effort it makes to comfort and reassure, to identify and define and to separate us from our fears. It would be easy, in this altered state, for the rage of self-protection, unopposed, to rise up and fight for all it's worth.

He sat still now, eyes averted, thinking. Only occasionally there were small erratic and impulsive movements, little lurches of the body, as if some underwater current were whipping him about.

How did you know? he asked.

Know what?

How did you know I was abused?

I didn't.

His eyes were wide now, soft with exposure. I didn't know, I said. I just wondered.

Well that's probably it, he said.

The moment swayed a little, outside itself, then returned.

We were in the presence of an opening, a clearing with an opportunity and a danger. Where to go? It would be wrong to pry open a path to a deep and painful experience and then leave it bleeding. Yet I worried he might have had enough. I decided that how we moved from here would depend on him.

Would you like to talk about it? I asked.

No.

Are you in therapy somewhere?

Yeah. For years. But we've never talked about this. I might not even have remembered it except that you asked.

Maybe it would be good to talk about it with your therapist.

For sure.

A feeling of equanimity came. Neither of us felt a need to speak. Enough for now, I thought. But I wanted to leave on a positive note.

I have an idea of what might make it easier if we have to do this again.

What?

To leave your conscious mind switched on.

How could we do that?

Without sedation.

He raised his eyebrows.

I know, you'd think the more the better. But this way you can stay in control. We could always add medications if we had to. But we've been that way, and frankly, the more we gave, the worse it got. Maybe this way you can talk to your subconscious mind and reassure it that no matter how horrible the experience feels and how much it resembles the ones that harmed you, it is *not* the same.

I went on: When I had my own endoscopy, I did it without sedation. It wasn't bad. Doctors are the worst patients imaginable. So you know that if I can do it, you can. Besides, it was convenient. I got right up and went back to work.

When the time came, and it did, that's how we did it. We hooked up an IV just in case he wanted to bail, used a little local benzocaine to numb down the throat, and selected the smallest possible pediatric scope so as to create the least disturbance. Meanwhile, I kept conversation going in which I talked him through every step of the way: Remember this is a scope with a light on it. This will only take a few minutes. You can tell me to stop any time you want to. Are you okay? We're getting a good look . . .

Not a ripple. There was no sign of the struggle we'd encountered before. And the news was good. The ulcer had healed and all signs of the offending bacteria had disappeared.

How did it go? I asked him in recovery.

No problem, was all he would say.

The effort must have fatigued him, for he dropped off

almost before finishing the sentence. As I sat watching him sleep, it came to me. That's it, I said to no one in particular: *Forbidden Planet*—the movie, the character Dr. Morbius, who, jealous of the young spaceship captain who would take his daughter away from him, imagined a monster to fight him off. The key was that the monster was known only to his subconscious mind and came to life when Dr. Morbius was sleeping, released into the moment when his conscious mind, the rational force, was not engaged to keep it in check. He was not *aware* of this monster. Denied by the conscious mind, it was orphaned and anonymous. But when the conscious mind was not in control, it lived ferociously. Billy had a Morbius Monster.

Billy got well and went away. I never saw him again. Maybe the experience was too much. Maybe he wanted to leave it behind. Maybe by recovering he no longer needed my services. Maybe his insurance changed. But Billy taught me something, and now I keep an eye out for the Morbius Monster and the sedation that makes it come to life.

Living It Up at the Top of the Mark

When he got the news, Tony went straight to the Mark Hopkins Hotel and rented the penthouse. He ordered Bay shrimp and Alaskan king crab. He drank martinis when he wasn't drinking Dom Pérignon. He rented ten pornographic videos and watched them all, back to back. He ate filet mignon. He stood at the window and grew nostalgic watching "the little cable cars, climb halfway to the stars." He allowed himself a chill watching the orange glow of sunset wash over the Golden Gate. In the evening he went to the Rockin' Rabbit Bar and Grill and picked up two floozies and fornicated his eyeballs out. By the end of the first day he'd racked up a $3,000 tab.

At noon the next day, when his Presidential Champagne Brunch had finished, the hotel manager knocked on his door. We're concerned, he said, through a fog of Cuban cigars, that you are maxing out your credit card.

No problem, said Tony, and handed him another. The manager smiled and backed out the door.

Tony's fellow students had no idea where he'd gone. He just didn't show for Friday's histology or pharmacology classes. By the time anatomy lab came around, everyone started asking questions.

A group of students formed a delegation and went to his roommate. What do you know? they asked.

Nothing, he said. He just wasn't in his bed this morning.

New girlfriend?

Not that I know of.

A singing telegram arrived at Tony's room, the kind that appears as a giant birthday cake rolled in on wheels. Tony had sent it to himself. The delivery service left the cake standing in the center of the room, and a gorgeous, topless, Marilyn Monroe look-alike named Brandy jumped out of the top and jiggled out a slightly off-tune melody that resembled something you might have heard before.

After three tunes and three unsuccessful attempts by Tony to get her in bed, she called for her horsemen, crawled into her carriage, and was wheeled to safety.

Tony decided to go down to the bar.

By Saturday morning the dean got involved. He found out that Tony had last been seen on campus Thursday afternoon in the dermatology clinic, but the attending dermatologist was in transit to Cairo for the annual international meetings and couldn't be reached.

The dean went to the computer and stole Tony's lab data and path report.

Sunday afternoon, in a stuporous cloud of alcohol and exhaustion, Tony got a call.

Hello, Tony?

Silence.

Tony, is that you? This is Dean Hammersmith.

Silence.

Tony, the police found your name on the hotel register. Are you ready to come home?

No, I don't think so.

Well, what are your plans?

I think I'll stay right here awhile.

Everybody's worried about you, Tony. The hotel isn't sure a starving medical student can pay off a seven-thousand-dollar bill.

Well, that's the point.

What's the point?

I won't *have* to pay it off.

The dean remained silent for a moment, pondering what he knew and what he didn't know. He decided to make Tony explain.

How do you figure that?

Tony paused. The dean thought he could hear the quick staccato of sucked-in breaths.

Dead people don't pay, he said.

The dean was silent. Pieces were falling in place, but the biggest piece was still missing.

Why do you think you're going to die?

Tony laughed the laugh that is part disgust at the ignorance of the question and part relief to be breaking into the subject with someone.

I've got melanoma, he said.

I know that, said the dean. I checked. But why do you think you're going to die?

It's metastasized.

Who told you?

I did. I mean, I *know*. I can tell.

How do you know?

Well . . .

The dean couldn't tell whether Tony was being dramatic or insecure.

I felt my liver.

And?

It's enlarged.

How large is it?

It's just at the margin. The right costal margin.

How far does it come down with inspiration?

Maybe a centimeter or two.

How high up is the upper border?

Silence.

Did you percuss out the upper border?

I forgot.

The dean put on his teaching hat. The liver is not enlarged unless the *span* of the liver is greater than eight to ten centimeters. It's common to feel a liver edge in young, thin people. It means nothing. If you're concerned about metastasis, we'll do a scan or something to find out, get a few blood tests . . .

Tony hung up the phone. He unplugged it from the wall. He had a lot to think about, but just now Jessica was arriving at his door, and that was a train of thought that couldn't be interrupted.

The dean waited until evening, had the maid service go in and plug in his phone.

Tony, he said.

Yeah.

Have you been thinking?

I have.

Do you still think you're about to die?

Yeah, probably. I mean, I don't know. Maybe not. Maybe not right away.

Don't you think it's time to come home?

No.

It's reached a critical point. Maybe a bit beyond critical.

I've been thinking about that . . .

But what?

I'm afraid.

What of?

I don't know. Suddenly it's all wrong. It's gone sour.

How about if I come downtown and take you home?

Tony went home. Had a good sleep. And got up for class the next day.

The dean kept secret what he knew and worked out a nice deal with the hotel. Tony went to work in the physiology lab to pay off some of the debt. The medical school paid some, and the hotel wrote off the rest.

Tony lived an untroubled life. The melanoma, but for its splash of melodrama, was gone from his body the day it was diagnosed and removed in the dermatology clinic.

One more ordeal faced him: Monday morning histology class. He wasn't sure how to play it: remorseful? repentant? foolish? So he didn't play it at all. He just showed up.

Maybe it was because he said nothing that things turned out the way they did — the nothing giving no apology and the no apology implying nothing to apologize for — for after the first twenty minutes or so, people started walking up to him, patting him on the back, or just nodding as if understanding was a form of grace that needed no explanation, something beyond explaining, not earned but given, like the little smile that began to form itself in the corner of his mouth.

Not Waving but Drowning

I've got a patient who can't tell me what her symptoms are, I said.

That's hard to imagine, she said.

The frustrating thing is it's hard to figure out what to do.

What does she say?

Well, she says, I had a terrible night.

That's all?

Just about. I ask her why it was terrible and she says, I'm not sure I can say.

My wife and I seldom have time to talk about my medical practice, but occasionally, after dinner, after the boys have gone off into the living room, there is a little clearing.

Is she confused?

She *says* she's confused. She says she's so anxious she can't stand it, yet she carries on conversations in other areas quite well.

What does she say about the nighttimes?

She doesn't. But in some vague way she seems to locate the problem in her stomach. So I ask her, Do you have any pain? And she says no. Any distention? No. Nausea? Indigestion? No. No. Any change in bowel habits? Yeah, but not much. The stools are "feathery" instead of formed, and she awakes with this urgency to have a BM but nothing comes.

What does that mean?

I don't know. Doesn't make sense. We checked her colon a few months ago when she said she was having some rectal bleeding. Nothing abnormal at all. And no bleeding. Besides, I've worked her up to the max for parasites, bacterial infection, toxins . . . all normal.

My wife looked that kind of look that tells me she's about to disagree with something I've said.

I think it's hard to describe what's going on in your own body. I had a hard time describing the pain of my ectopic pregnancy, and that was a *big deal*.

How come?

I just couldn't put it into words.

Why not?

I don't know, maybe because I'm not trained to think that way, maybe . . . a dream . . .

What do you mean, a dream?

There was a long silence. See, pain is hard to describe. I can't even describe how it feels to *describe* my pain.

She played with her napkin. All I could say was that I wanted to get in a certain position and stay there. That was the best I could do.

She paused, moved her fork along the tablecloth but didn't pick it up. Is she for real?

Hard to tell. She has a long history of psychiatric problems, largely depression, and she's acting very confused. Last time she was in the office, I thought about asking her to check in with her psychiatrist, but I don't feel too good about that.

Why not?

Well, she's lost ten pounds. She's at an age when she might drop a few pounds without anything being wrong, but you have to take seriously anyone who's lost weight.

Does she have a primary doctor?

Yeah, they've tinkered with her thyroid, but she didn't put back the pounds. I went over to see him yesterday and told him his patient was driving me crazy. I was worried something was wrong, but I couldn't get a handle on it.

My wife looked quizzical. Isn't she the one who calls you all the time?

Yeah. Same thing over and over. She can't keep her medications straight. So I went over to Doctor Malhoney's office and got a list of everything he'd ordered, wrote it down myself, clearly, added my list to his list, and presented it to her. Then she called me the minute she got home to ask about her medications.

Didn't she call here at seven o'clock last Saturday morning?

She did. She can't seem to remember what I say. We've had the same conversation four times already this week.

Maybe it's Alzheimer's.

The day after my conversation with my wife, my patient called and made an emergency appointment. Well, I'm very unhappy, she said.

Let's find out why.

I don't know where to start.

Anywhere you like.

I took that Zelnorm — it was awful — it didn't do anything.

That was for when you were having constipation. Maybe it caused too many contractions of the bowel?

Anyway, I took only four of them.

But *why* was it you stopped?

I can't recall. Well, let me tell you what I did. I took the Metamucil, how much I don't recall, and then I didn't have a movement. I stopped it Sunday night. Definitely. I had made up my mind I would never take another of those Metamucil pills.

Why not?

Just let me finish. I had breakfast at eight a.m. And I took a suppository and had a little BM. But yesterday, two doses of Metamucil and that was it. Then I went out to dinner and did a foolish thing. I ate split-pea soup, and I had a wonderful salad of spinach, carrots, and a little butter lettuce. It was wonderful. What happened, really, I had the runs. I'm sorry, but really that's what happened.

What caught my attention was her smile as she described the salad. Doesn't sound like a foolish thing to me.

I have it here, and I definitely saw spinach.

She reached in her purse and pulled out a napkin wrapped in clear plastic.

It took me a minute to realize what was going on. I gathered my wits and took the specimen from her. I performed a little test for blood, which added drama to the situation and which was negative. Then I combed through it with a wooden probe and saw no undigested foods.

It seems normal.

But I get scared.

Let me examine your belly.

I did that. Her abdomen was soft and non-tender. There were no masses and no enlarged organs. The bowel sounds were normal.

Things are not going well, I said. I think we need to push further to see that we don't miss something. It's difficult to know what to do when the symptoms — and I paused to say that I did not blame her for this — when the symptoms are so nonspecific. I know you've had a colonoscopy within the last six months, but I propose repeating that and getting a CT scan of your abdomen.

Next day she called to say she couldn't get to sleep the night before.

Why?

I don't know why.

A harmless parasite appeared in one of her stool specimens. I discussed it with her and decided to give her medications for it on the off chance it might be responsible for some of her urgency at night. Likewise, we might try an anti-inflammatory for the bowel. These were long shots, and I told her so, but maybe worth a try.

In three days she stopped both medicines because they made her feel strange.

I walked over to her primary doctor's office, and I told him we weren't making any progress and that I had decided to push out the perimeter of the workup to see if something else was going on.

We've done a CT scan and had a colon scheduled, but she canceled. I was beginning to worry that she was decompensating. Did she have a psychiatrist?

Yes. I'll send her over.

CT scan. CT scan, I said to myself on the way back to my office. I couldn't decide if I'd done it yet.

I checked the chart. It wasn't there. Shit. I thought we'd done that two weeks ago.

Let's schedule a CT, I said to my office staff, almost at the level of a shout.

Christmas was upon us. She called to ask if she could go to her sister's in Sonoma for the holidays.

No reason not to, I said.

I gave her my number in case she got in trouble, and she called the minute she arrived.

I'm confused about my medications, she said.

Which ones?

All of them. I just can't get it straight. When we were

done I asked to speak to her sister to make sure someone knew what to do.

Back from the holidays, and a new set of lab tests was on my desk. The alkaline phosphatase was elevated.

Oh my God, I said. I've seen this before. Some sneaky something growing in the liver can elevate this enzyme.

I walked out to the front desk to tell someone to call her right away, and she was standing at my elbow.

I was wondering if I could talk to you for a few minutes, she said.

Yes, and right now. Come with me.

We went to the exam room. I told her about the test, and that I was worried something might be growing somewhere.

I have something to show you.

She lifted her blouse and pointed to a little nodule just above her belly button.

Christ, I said to myself. That's the Sister Mary Joseph sign.

I hadn't thought of that term in years, but I remembered the lecture in medical school. Sister Mary Joseph was a very wise and intelligent nurse who observed that patients dying of cancer sometimes had little hard nodules on their abdomens, in a curious location around the navel. These little stones accreting in the wall turned out to be cancer metastasis to the lymph node left behind when mother and child separated. It was a terminal condition. The good sister even developed a little reputation making dire but accurate predictions when she spotted her sign.

I called in my associate to confirm my opinion. He concurred.

I pictured a huge cancer socked in the pelvis, pressing on the bowel.

Because of the holidays, the CT scan hadn't been scheduled until the following day, and the colon exam the day after. We gave her the detailed instructions, emphasizing the importance of following through.

I have to tell you this, she said. Maybe I shouldn't say anything, but your receptionist always leaves me on hold for a long time.

This was a break into a new sense of camaraderie. She'd never talked about things like this before. She had been emboldened by our common and newly elevated concern for her welfare.

I was thinking of the five times she called each day and how this had the effect of exasperating even the best of us. I'm sorry, I said. We are all concerned about you and want very much to get to the bottom of this.

I noticed she wore a bright smile. Things were happening, activity was rising up and circling about her. She seemed at ease. She was being listened to.

That night I gave my wife an update.

This kind of story always makes you want to do every test imaginable, right off the bat, she said.

Right. And I had that impulse. But if I did that every time, I'd be ordering a lot of normal tests.

Neither of us was satisfied with that.

I tried again. If I put "I don't feel right" or "I can't get to sleep" as the reason for the test, the insurance company would bounce it right back.

What do they have to do with it?

Nowadays they insist upon granting prior authorization for a lot of tests. Primarily the expensive ones. You have to say the right buzzword or it won't happen.

Can't you just do it anyway?

It won't get paid for. And that's a powerful, all-but-absolute deterrent. Besides, Radiology won't even schedule a CT scan without a prior authorization number.

During the silence that followed, I was thinking that a few weeks one way or the other would probably not affect the outcome, but still, we all could have been on the right track a lot sooner.

And I tried to imagine what it must be like to announce your difficulty and not be heard. It reminded me of the Stevie Smith poem "Not Waving but Drowning." Signals offered in the wrong language. Meaning lost in the interpretation.

Why do you suppose you didn't order the CT scan? my wife asked.

I don't know. And I shook my head with a little chuckle of admiration for her marksmanship, always landing squarely upon the issue.

Part of me would say I was distracted by the camouflage.

Go on.

Part of me says the system wouldn't have allowed the right tests anyway.

My wife just watched me squirm.

Yeah, right. It's a signal that I didn't take her seriously enough.

Neither of us needed to talk about outcomes or the anguish my patient felt, not waving but drowning. We knew which could be helped and which could not. There was just a little moment in which we thought good thoughts for her, almost like the quick breath of a poem or a prayer. Then we picked up our forks and finished dinner.

Annie's Antidote

The fear that thumps us down. That's what made her wait so long. Annie, the mild-mannered piano teacher, was fearful, so fearful that everything concerning her health required negotiation. In the moment when her clear thinking told her what to do, she lost courage, as if friendly forces suddenly withdrew to a foreign country.

Fear sucked her energy like a power outage. Mention the word *endoscopy* and she turned pale, her eyes drifting off like somebody unplugged.

Three months already, we should have done her endoscopy. First-choice treatments have their reasons. When fear takes them out, we drift into seconds, hoping the difference is not so great as to mislead or, worse, do harm. So we shifted back to medicines instead, added some alternatives, switched around the timing . . .

Fear fought us even there. Just the thought of side effects made taking medicines seem like injecting poison into the body, a grave contamination that could upset the fragile balance of life, or what passed for life, clinging to the narrow edge.

Through all this, the pesky symptoms stayed on, and on. It was they that finally forced us to stare into the face of fear.

I guess we all have fears: flying thirty-seven thousand feet over the Atlantic Ocean in a bullet-shaped projectile with wings glued on, propelling straight up a small chamber sixty stories to your accountant's office, driving over countless tons of steel delicately suspended, God knows how many feet over the tidewaters of the Golden Gate, to get to work every morning — it's a wonder we don't all run around in a state of abject terror. Most of us have developed ways of not thinking about it. We can't afford to, in a life that requires one long, continuous leap of faith.

So we make peace with fear. Or we reach a point of necessity that says, Screw it, just do what you have to do.

But sometimes the weight of the hammer that breaks us free has to be pretty great. So I'm not too surprised when people put off coming to see me. All too often it requires something drastic, an uncle dying of stomach cancer, a young friend. Then comes the realization: Well, maybe I'd better go get that endoscopy.

But Annie was in that phase where everything negative was magnified, empowered. Anxiety like this changes the playing field. Great terrors rise to besiege and paralyze — something as simple as a dental appointment or crossing the desert by car — an event that to others might seem ordinary can send the anxious to apoplexy.

We had postponed ourselves into a tight spot and quite possibly transformed a simple disease into a complicated one.

She realized, eventually, she couldn't afford her fears. So with great courage she accepted the reality that this thing was going to happen, scheduled an appointment, and made herself go. Made herself actually show up.

But as we were waiting to begin, she freaked.

She had brought her Walkman and her favorite music to calm her, but it failed. Now, she trembled on the table as if shot through by voltage.

I can't do it, she said.

And everything stopped.

I knew better than to force it. So we just waited, sitting around, trying to decide what to do, me on the little stool with wheels, the nurse leaning against the cabinet on the opposite wall, everybody taking a little time to breathe.

Some time went by.

She seemed to struggle with her body. It wanted to leave, lurching occasionally as if to leap from the table in a brief outburst of force that was just as quickly neutralized or tied down by the counterforce of her will.

Finally she said, You're a poet, aren't you?

I was startled. Where had that thought come from, and what was it doing here? But I didn't dare question anything that might move us along some new path, *any* direction from where we were.

Guilty as charged, I said.

She laughed. The tension in the room seemed to relax. Maybe if you said a poem to me, I could go through with this.

It was an opening, however unusual. And a spell was weaving around us in which it seemed we had started working together on something, a project perhaps, something that sapped the spotlight from its fixation upon impasse.

I think so, I said, and flipped through the pages of my memory. But I'm afraid I only know one poem. It's one of my own I memorized to say at a poetry festival a long time ago.

Could I hear it?

I leaned back, took a deep breath, waited long enough for my head to shift over into a different world, and recited:

> *My son brings me a stone*
> *and asks which star*
> *it fell from. He is serious*
> *so I must be careful, even though*
> *I know he will place it among those things*
> *that will leave him someday*
> *and he will go on gathering,*
> *for this is one of those moments*
> *that turns suddenly towards you, opening*
> *as it turns, as if we paused*

on the edge of a heartbeat and then pressed
forward, conscious
of the fear that runs beside us
and how lovely it is to be with each other
in the long resilient mornings.

In the silence that followed, it was clear to me that whatever power I had to change anything about this situation had been spent. Our direction had been cast, only as yet it remained unknown to me. Whatever was to happen, I thanked my good luck that the only poem I knew by heart seemed to suggest a certain resiliency of the human spirit that rose from — from what? — perhaps just from the companionship we share in the face of joy . . . or loss. Companionship. Well, at least we've got that.

She was silent. She seemed about to speak several times before she finally gave us a start:

I'm ready, she said. And lay down.

I moved quickly. Five minutes and we were done. The procedure went without a hitch. The biopsy from the edge of her ulcer revealed the infection, *Helicobacter pylori,* and some antibiotics cleared up the whole thing. Her long and troublesome struggle with symptoms became a thing of the past. Nice outcome. Nice and timely accomplishment for her. She triumphed — and it felt that way to all of us concerned. Thereafter, she seemed charged with a higher wattage of confidence. Her posture improved.

And I wondered what exactly it was that called off her

demon, or at least stunned it long enough for us to do our thing. What turned her from wuss to warrior? Something told her that hidden within the hearing of a poem was the thing she needed. Was it a message of hope? Of resiliency? Of an experience that somehow shone through a rude reminder of mortality? Maybe the music was strong enough to soothe the rhythms of the body. Maybe she just felt more confident knowing her doctor was human.

I don't know. But she found a little something to put in her pocket to place the monster on hold. And on top of that, no side effects. What drug could be better?

I've thought about it, but I've given up trying to figure it out. I realize it's mystery, and love the word. And love that mystery still works in our lives.

MRS. ROBINSON EYES

He said he was sorry to disturb me at 2:00 a.m., but he thought a faculty member should be involved. James was one of our better gastroenterology trainees, and I always figured he could handle most anything.

Why do you need me?

Because my patient is my colleague. She's a third-year surgery resident.

He told me that she was getting ready to go on a backpacking trek and at the last moment her girlfriend finked out. Danielle was home packing by herself when she started to vomit blood.

Hematemesis is a sign of a major problem — ulcer, perhaps, or severe gastritis. Still, James could have handled it — except for the colleague thing. It meant I had to travel across town in the middle of the night, but I saw the need. I said I'd be right there.

We did what we are trained to do: sedation, endoscopy, the search for the source. All went well except that no sign of bleeding was found. Blood, yes. But no *bleeding* — and no ulcer, no varix, no gastritis . . . nothing.

It happens like that sometimes. Wouldn't you know, it would have to be another doctor. All the same, this one, like all the others, would sort itself out in time.

She was transfused, she recovered, she reentered society, that is, what passes for society in a surgical residency. And we heard nothing more until a couple of months later.

Same drill. This time occurring in the wake of her mother's visit. Blood transfusions, lab tests, X-rays — and no source found. Things were looking strange. I reminded myself they often do, when dealing with members of the medical profession.

There was talk of surgical exploration. The interns were restless. The attending physicians were uncomfortable with the uncertainty of no diagnosis in someone who continued to have episodic bleeding. I was impatient, too, but I told them I don't do fishing expeditions. And on top of that, no answer pre-op is better than no answer post-op.

She seemed to thrive in the hospital. She endeared herself to the medical staff, who generally felt sorry for her, but she managed to alienate the nurses with her high-maintenance demands — long talks, the insatiable need for the little things.

I was not pleased. The momentum was building for surgery. Even the consultants felt it might be a means of examining parts of the bowel that our proddings and zappings had left uncharted.

I said no surgery until I get psychiatric clearance, and I brought the best psychiatrist I could find. He reported that she was an attractive, intelligent young woman with no psychiatric problem.

We went to surgery.

The surgeon removed part of the upper small bowel because that was the area most under suspicion. On pathological exam, everything was normal. I was beginning to think we had created our own worst nightmare. The old surgical adage popped to mind: Whoever creates a monster has to take care of it. But then surgeons were notorious for not following their patients. The monster gets passed back to the internist.

The bleeding stopped after surgery, but she developed gastric outlet obstruction, a post-op complication in which no food passes out of the stomach. This required a second surgery to open up a channel into the small bowel. I counted the minutes until the next disaster.

She leveled off awhile. By now I knew about her schizophrenic mother, who was the CEO of a major chemical company. I knew about her receding, alcoholic father who was too wimpy or too sloshed to give the children much support. I knew about the emotional famine of her early years, how her mother's criticism entered her like a violation, how the only way she could get the slightest sign of affection was to get As on her report card or get sick. I concluded she had become proficient at both.

She made dolls for my children, had crystal sent from Germany, teas from China. She was in my house, among my family, settling in. I came home to find her lying on my living room sofa, waited upon by my wife . . . a little warm broth, a box of Kleenex, perhaps some soda from the corner store . . .

We had a conversation. I told her she was to limit the extent of her illness. I was certain she could do it, and if I was to continue as her physician, I expected it.

Two months went by without a ripple. Then I got a call from the ER. The nurse told me that Danielle had pleaded with them not to bother me, but she had become so weak that as a last resort she just had to come to the ER. They discovered a dangerously low blood potassium, the lowest they'd ever seen. For some reason the image of Mrs. Robinson in *The Graduate* popped into mind — that scene in which she discovers her lover is having an affair with her daughter — the wide camera angle, black dress, white walls looming larger as the camera pulls back. The look in her eyes that has become the look in Danielle's eyes. *That* posture. *That* isolation.

Potassium is basic. It's in cells, in blood — moves in through the gastrointestinal tract and out through the kidneys. There are not many places it can hide, not many aberrations that will cause such a dramatic depletion. The nurse said they were admitting her to my service. After a week of blood tests and consultations, we still didn't know what was happening. And the potassium stayed low.

The weekend came. Her mother was in town on a visit. Danielle demanded a pass. Passes are not given. If you can be out on pass, you don't need to be in a hospital.

But she was insistent in a desperate way I had never seen before, as if the conclusion were foregone — as if all that remained was to force beyond whatever stood in the way, no matter what. She was out in a flash.

A few hours later she returned. Any trace of desperation was gone. Her potassium, which had been creeping back to normal, was down again. I made a few calls. I reached her mother at home. Yes, Danielle was in a very strange mood that day. They ran errands. Went to a pharmacy.

A pharmacy?

Yes, she had to fill a prescription.

It was Saturday evening, but I had the pharmacist on the phone in ten minutes. Yes, he had filled a prescription for her. It was Lasix. Lasix, a strong diuretic that sweeps potassium out of the kidneys like crazy. Who signed the prescription?

Everything came clear, bursting open, spreading out and sinking in like water over sand. Part of me couldn't imagine such a thing and had struggled to keep me from discovering the truth. Another part had known it all along. That part was now feeling triumphant. It made me feel strangely excited, powerful. I went back to the hospital. She was surprised to see me.

I know where you went today.

No response.

I know you filled a prescription for Lasix. You forged my name.

No response.

That's what made you lose so much potassium. You've been taking that to fool us. You must have run out and panicked.

Silence was a gel in the air of the room.

Out loud I wondered if even the bleeding was self-induced. I asked her point-blank.

Silence.

I was remembering some reference to a crumpled-up transfusion bag in the wastebasket of her apartment. Was it my imagination? Was it her roommate who'd told me? Was that information just too improbable to be believed?

As a physician she would have known how much blood to take out and when to stop. But the part that required a giant leap was that she would then have had to swallow her own blood. It was hard to imagine.

I called the psychiatrist. We've got a problem here, I told him. You'd better take another look.

Things went orbital. She developed meningitis, pneumonia, urinary-tract infections, several kinds of bacteria growing in her blood at the same time — I imagined her injecting herself with fecal material, but could never catch her at it. I began to have a strange admiration for her talent, how she walked the tightrope between life and death with immaculate skill. It was desperation elevated to an art form.

Each time she was admitted to the hospital, the house staff would get agitated after a few days. We'll never get her out of here, they'd say. Just watch, I told them. I'd walk into the room, sit on the edge of the bed, and say, Danielle, I'm going to discharge you in thirty-six hours. You'd better be well by then. And I'd leave the room. And she would be well. Fevers defervesced, septicemias cleared, rashes resolved, meningitis went away, and she walked out as if nothing had happened, whole, intact, steady.

It was the nurses who were trapped, caught between their desire to relieve suffering and the clear perspective from the bedside that questioned Danielle's illness. They suffered a schizophrenia of thought and deed. Picture a volcano crater, I told them. Imagine standing on the rim, tossing small pebbles into the center. You'll never fill her need. Fine, they said, but what's wrong with her? I said, She has Mrs. Robinson eyes.

I learned which moments to let ceremony continue and which openings I could take that would steer it to conclusion. I became the visiting expert, the magician from a foreign country called in to cast out the spell.

In time she drifted away. I supposed that the balance between what I knew of the secrets about her and what I could do to help eventually tipped into the red zone and she had to go. She needed freedom to drift in and out of care without the weight of history dragging her down. For when that part of her rose with its Mrs. Robinson eyes, she had to have a place that would give it what it demanded, a small emergency room perhaps, a protected place somewhere deep in the night, where the patient like a map could spread herself on the table, open and hungry for the close attention of physicians, who, like cartographers with their needles, scopes, and scalpels, would touch her in a way that almost felt like love.

ECTOPIC

How is it going to die? That was her question.

The obstetrician looked like he'd never thought about that before, and took a moment to recover.

Her husband remembered their first night, how they fell so easily together, how for a moment the next morning they thought she might be pregnant. He encountered there her first flash of opinion: no pill, no abortion, absolutely not.

By first light they had a history.

By now there had been multiple attempts to get pregnant, followed by the news they'd missed their chance. FSH too high. Eggs old before their time. The irony was inescapable. Microsurgery, hormones, the long waitings suffused with waves of apprehension, hope, and despair—and now, after several attempts at in vitro fertilization, a sudden pain in the ninth week and there are two pregnancies, one in its perfect path, one crimped in a barren tube.

I guess by cautery, the doctor said. That's how we open the tube.

No one said a word. It will be instantaneous, he added, in a tone meant to reassure.

If it was a gesture of reassurance, it was passed over. The full weight of her thinking was on the next decision: spinal or general. Spinal would be painful when they tipped her up to free the pelvic organs. All that air in the belly. All that pressure against the diaphragm. But general might endanger the other pregnancy. She had no hesitation. It would have to be spinal.

There was hardly a ripple of the first night in this one. He nuzzled back into the small space on the periphery of the imagination from which he had just stepped forward to encourage and support, back to where he only observed, conscious now, how the playing surface changes the game — peritonitis would set in, both the mother and the other child might loose their lives — how we are not given rules like these until the championship game, our only certainty the will to keep playing.

His glances to the past for wisdom had found none there. He was in the present and in this disconnected present he had a wife on the operating table and a good embryo in the womb's heart. Certain confusions fall away in the presence of that.

It was late, past midnight, in the hours long after the work of the day had passed and there was a soft hum of space into which all the irregular and unappropriated could be placed. Laparoscopy. Suction. The strained, thin blood of the overexhausted drawn into waste and discarded. And with it, that which was alive until now.

It remained only to wait in that quiet arrangement of suspension so familiar to them by now, made for events one could not expect nor control to play out, not made but mandated, in which there is no accounting for the separation they feel from time: the OR emptying itself of its scheduled cases, the anesthesiologist making ready, the pendulum, deliberate in its swing.

He could do no more than to love these lives, flourishing in the afterglow of a night that had launched them with no backward glances, and to love the life that was fading away, her name not yet spoken into the resilience of the world.

ME AND THE HEC

The person at the Human Experimentation Committee said my study sounded simple enough — just give a few poems to people about to have surgery and see if it calmed them down some. He said it should pass through on the *expedited* path — not have to go through the whole committee — and would I please go online and take this little test to see if I knew enough about the current regulations.

I just wanted to give my patients a few poems, so I wrote up this little description about what I planned to do and bundled it up and sent it away, and I went online and took that little test . . .

Three weeks, and a letter comes that says the full committee has to review this study of mine and my consent form needs to be two consent forms in order to accommodate all the new regulations — and by the way, did I take that little test yet?

I said I had, and my name was posted right up there on his Web site with all the others who had taken his test — and they wanted to know why did I think poetry might calm anybody down . . .

So I told him the story about my patient who freaked out on the table and who, after we sat around twiddling our thumbs awhile, wanted to know if I'd recite her a poem.

I did that.

And she lay right down and had her surgery. Just like that.

Three weeks, and I get it all back — they said they didn't understand how I meant to compare those blood pressures I meant to compare, and I thought it sounded a little like the Department of Defense asking Lockheed for a business plan — but I figured they were just trying to teach me something about clear thinking when it comes to comparing blood pressures . . . So I went to the biostatistics guy and he asked me why did I think poetry might have an effect in the first place.

And I said, Let's skip to the numbers . . .

So the guy wrote up some fancy formulae that signified we'd thought about the problem and might even have ascended to the level of clear thinking (in thirty-two pages in a ten-point font), and I hadn't given a single poem to a single person yet.

It was a good experience, the way they made me think about things I'd never thought about before that may have saved some hardship for somebody about to be abused by a poem somewhere.

And the news is we finally did get that approval. Conditional, it was . . .

If I'd just go online and take that little test.

PALOOKA

She came to my office with a husband and a son. I need an internist, she said.

That would be me, I said.

Extra people are sometimes useful. The patient can be so nervous her circuits get overloaded and she may not hear things right. But it can also mean there is an abiding distrust of doctors or maybe a personal character flaw she hopes to override by plurality. Something about the theatrical way she paused before speaking, something about the way she looked to make sure her entourage was at full attention, made me lean in the direction of the flaw.

I've got a lot of problems, she said, raising one eyebrow to warn me.

Here we go. So far we're on track with my instincts. In the early going, my job was shaping up to this: be of service and don't be easy to scare off.

I've had some pretty complicated patients, I said. And if

something comes up I can't handle, I'll find someone who can. And I'm thinking to myself that I really do want to be of service to this woman. I just have a tendency to analyze as I go along.

I feel better already, she said.

I was pleased, but thought her comfort was a little too easy. More important, I thought, would be how she felt at the *end* of the visit.

I'm having surgery tomorrow, she said. And I'm nervous.

Tomorrow. Jesus! One day from surgery and I'll be called upon to ascend to a state of instant familiarity and wisdom about someone I've just met.

Then we'd better get busy, I said.

You see the bandage on my nose.

It was a Joe Palooka bandage. I couldn't have missed it. It was the kind cartoonists draw to depict big-time failure in the ring the night before. Anything that obvious had to be of pivotal importance.

At the mention of the word *bandage,* the son reached over and patted her forearm.

Her husband spoke. I'd like you to know, Doctor, she's been through a lot. She's nervous. She's not herself. She's really a very different person from what you see today. More patting. I realized, all this time, I hadn't learned a thing about her illness.

Maybe someone could give me a little history, I said.

You see, Doctor, she began, I've got . . .

And at this point she sort of slumped in the chair and

looked helplessly off to the side. Air escaped from her mouth, luffing the upper lip like a deflating rubber balloon. As I watched the two men turn in toward her like petals over a wilting stamen, a strange sense of frustration, almost impatience, came over me. I wasn't sure why I felt this way. After all, this is my work environment. People come to me all the time with emotions on their sleeves, and I understand, I accept, and I don't let it bother me.

Her husband finished the sentence: She has cancer of her nose. She can't bring herself to say the word.

Oh. Sorry to hear that.

But it worried me that she couldn't bring herself to say the C-word. It has always seemed to me that patients who take an assertive, self-protective, shall we say almost combative posture, do better than those for whom depression or dependency slows down the clockwork. We didn't have time to go into the psychiatry of it. I needed rudiments.

She gained strength to speak again: I've got this awful hole. You *will* be my doctor, won't you?

I think you're stuck with me, I said. And I threw in a little smile. It felt a little like we were becoming friends. And I scolded myself. Who was I to judge this person's emotions? This lady was coming to me with a stinking-awful cancer on the end of her nose, a repulsive and dangerous aberration apt to disfigure her greatly before it was done. Wasn't she entitled to be a little overwhelmed? I was overreacting. But I was also aware that no evidence of my argument with myself would escape to the surface. It wasn't that

I was hiding something; I was just responding at two separate levels, one of which was invisible, both genuine. Fur-
thermore, these observations would not drag on my desire
to help this lady. I would be her doctor, follow her through
surgery, be available for her questions . . . and do this feeling no restraint on passion or respect.

I already like you, she said.

I didn't feel very worthy, but despite my best efforts a
rather undeserved rush of pleasure swept through me.

The husband made a gesture that indicated the hole was
substantial and the repair would be extreme. Three years
ago she had had a small lesion on her nose shaved off. That's
okay for well-behaved cancers. Not this one, it appeared,
which had leapfrogged over neighboring cells. Now she had
to have a wide excision.

I said I understood her fear, but there were at least two
points in her favor. As surgeries go, this one wasn't life-
threatening. And because I guessed she needed proof, I
made a short list of horrendous surgeries to locate her
at a more reasonable point on the curve of perspective. I
guessed she wouldn't stay reassured very long, but I forged
ahead anyway. And if you have to have it done, I said, you've
got the best surgeon to do it. I know him personally, and
he's first-rate.

It was true, what I said, but it was also very good for confidence. And it was working. I could see it flicker in the
quick gesture of her hand, her back straightening up from a
slouch. To nail this I would have to go one step further.

I leaned over and looked her in the eye. You'll come through this okay, I said. And I knew as I said it that no one could know that. But you can't just spew out numbers and odds like a computer. Especially for this person, who was more likely to be moved by the wisdom of my gut than the computations of my brain.

Statistics can be harmful. If you tell a patient she has a 0.5 percent chance of dying, *all* she hears is "dying." Mix in a little neurosis or too much stress, and the word enters her so fully she believes she's just received a death sentence.

And she would be painfully afraid of death. If she couldn't say the word *cancer,* she sure wasn't going to say *death.*

I think I can say the surgery won't kill you, I said, offering the little smile that says, We all know that's obvious but it feels good to say it anyway.

You're a nice man, she said.

Not so nice, I said. But I would not challenge her further. I knew that soon enough too much praise can turn into too much rage. I was in her world now, and somehow it served her to think well of me.

Let's make a list, I said.

I have one. Where is it? Oh dear, I can't find it. Husband and son groped in her purse, pockets, backpack, and eventually produced a small piece of paper:

1. Back pain — I need a pillow between my knees when lying on my side.

2. Pillow at back.
3. Control over pain meds — I changed my mind from when I talked to the anesthesiologist.
4. Fungus in mouth — is it related to antibiotics?
5. Antibiotics: currently taking for sinus infection — what to do?
6. Will you talk to the surgeon?
7. And the anesthesiologist?
8. No interns asking questions.

I'm not sure about that last one, I said. This is a teaching hospital, and one of the big reasons people come here is the brain trust that collects at university centers. The trade-off is that you may have to put up with extra interviews and examinations, but overall it's a bargain. Besides, you underestimate the interns and students — they're smart and well trained, and sometimes they pick up key bits of information that have a significant effect upon outcome.

I don't want them to touch me.

Doctor Markbreit will do the surgery, if that's what you're worried about. But if we are to train the super-docs of the future, they have to at least be in the vicinity.

I've heard horror stories.

From who?

Friends.

I don't know what it is about "friends," I said, that makes them scare the hell out of people. I laughed, but she didn't.

Let me give you an example, I said. I do colonoscopies practically every day. It's a simple procedure. I can always tell when someone has paid attention to bad advice. They're frightened and their blood pressure is on the ceiling. They get all worked up over nothing, and when it's done the best they can do is ask if I've started yet. It's mostly piss and bluster. As it turns out, interns are pretty nice people. Give 'em a chance. You'll probably end up liking them a lot.

Oh, all right, but will you personally talk to the anesthesiologist?

Now don't worry about the stuff you shouldn't worry about. If you or I were calling the shots for the anesthesiologists, we'd all be in deep doo-doo.

But how will I know everything is okay?

Because I'll tell you, that's how.

A little silence followed in which I reflected upon how I might have been a little rough. Maybe not rough but blunt, blunt with a little extra weight for effect. There was no time to convince her by the usual time-consuming pathway of reason and trust. She would have to be carried on charisma until we had time for confidence.

Come on, Elaine, I said. You need to get a move on. I've still got to listen to your heart and lungs, take a blood pressure—you know—check you over a bit and scribble down all that stuff that will make this happen.

She was crying.

Anticipation is worse than the event, I said.

I can't cry.

Maybe it's good for you.

No, I mean it gets in my bandage.

We all laughed.

Scut work now: record the physical exam, fax it to the hospital, get the lab work done, call the surgeon:

Saw Elaine, I said.

Oh my God, thanks a lot.

She has a list of requests.

Shoot.

He took it pretty well. All but the part about no anti-biotics.

Have to, he said. If I lay fresh tissue down on a front yard of bacteria, it's just going to lift right off again.

Well, you'd better give her some kind of antifungal lozenge to suck on, then.

Fine, he said. And I can keep the interns pretty quiet. I guess I owe you for this one.

Yes, you do. And I won't let you forget it.

Two days later I got a call that she was being discharged from the hospital and wanted to see me. She was having problems with her sense of taste. I was a little embarrassed I hadn't been to see her after her surgery. The thought occurred to me I'd been avoiding her. Then it hit me. She was a carbon copy of my mother—not physically but emo-tionally—her practiced skill to collapse in the vicinity of help, the sideward glance, the need for rescue, her failure before the word *cancer,* the clutch of support that seemed so necessary and moved with her like rings and rings of undulating petticoats.

I called it manipulation when I was growing up, a word I used to place the impact a safe distance from me, a way of naming and thus gaining a sense of mastery over the machinery that could set expectations and wield guilt, and that had had such a controlling effect on my life. I always thought I was more than willing to give support. What got to me was the *expectation*.

Not going to see her until now stirred the same kind of little lie I might have used with my mother. I would tell Elaine I thought she had already been discharged. I hated that but was glad to dodge the bullet. Face it. I was a child again.

When I arrived, seven people were in the room: the nurse, the discharge social worker, the family I had met before and some I hadn't. Everyone seemed to be having a good time. The father and son were in nifty gray suits, looking like they'd just stepped out of Macy's front window.

I delivered my lie that everyone expected and accepted as part of the game.

Well, in a way I *was* already gone, she said. One foot in the other world. I guess I've been there and back.

Opening gambit a success: knight to bishop three. We were now in midgame.

I examined her tongue. It was flat. The little papillae denuded. Probably yeast from all those antibiotics, I said. Taste buds got scared away. They'll be back.

They will? Oh, I like the sound of that.

The husband asked if the surgeons might have accidentally cut the nerve.

No. No. They weren't in that area at all. Let's pick the simpler explanation. It has a better outcome.

Oh, I like that, she said. Let's take that one. The family and nurses all nodded and smiled.

I'm seeing another side of you, I said, something I've not seen before. You're actually . . . pesky. Perky.

Yes, and I'd like to thank you.

Don't thank me. I didn't do much.

Yes, you did. You said you'd take care of me, and that means a lot. You don't hear that very often these days.

I was now witness to the other side of my mother, the part I admired and tried my best to copy: gracious, benevolent, quick to compliment, genuinely concerned about the welfare of others, and very, very proud of her family. There was conviviality, and—how should I say it—I was having fun.

I was struck with the irony of the struggle I had had with her manner while at the same time she was showering me with praise. She was a nice person. My struggle was not with her. It was with myself.

I moved toward the door and changed the subject. You look like you're ready for the cotillion, my dear, maybe a coming-out party.

Yes. I'll write the Clintons and invite them.

We were in the hall now. The family, as I knew they would, followed me. They asked the same questions I had already answered. It wasn't about answers. It was a little ritual called We Are Showing Concern. It could have been irritating, but I knew they were doing what they were doing because of how well it worked to hold things together.

Meet my other son, the father said. The son was dressed in a leather jacket, open collar, pleasantly unkempt linen slacks. He was leaning against the wall in the shadows off to the side, and after shaking hands, he separated himself again from the group. This one I recognized as the rebellious one. I knew in a flash how he felt, so I made a point of making eye contact with him, to signal, perhaps, a confederacy of sorts. He, I imagined, showed his struggle by acting out, as my younger brother did, and then paid for it later.

I walked down the hall with a sense of closure. She had been witty and gracious, not at all the clingy, needy person of three days ago. The husband was right to say she was not herself when she first visited me. At least not the self she was now. The surgery was over. She'd made it.

She had triumphed.

A month later I ran across Dr. Markbreit in the hall by the emergency room. How's Elaine? I asked.

That reminds me, he said, I've got to call her. You know, the initial biopsies were all read as negative, and I went ahead and started the reconstruction that would become her new nose. Now they tell me they're all positive. It means I've got to go back in there, take down all that work, take the skin back to the skull, and start over. It's going to be a big deal.

His words split me in two. My medical part already had the details of the next pathway worked out. I could hear that part speaking from my mouth, discussing the case with Dr. Markbreit. The other part was shaken. Maybe like hearing the news about a member of your own family.

All that optimism I spewed forth to get us to the table — how would she see it now? As support? As betrayal? Or did she understand it was all part of the game we play to get the earnest work done?

I imagined her hearing the news. She would have to go through, all over again, the terrors her fear would bring and the cascade it would send shuddering down through the family. She would say she couldn't do it. Her family would rally around her, encouraging her, patting her on the arm as she stayed away as long as she could, and finally, on the last day before surgery, she would come and see me again.

I would be ready this time. I would recognize her. I would recognize myself.

Her Language

I'd like to be better at it, she said. I'd like to read how other people do it so I can be perfect.

Sondra is about twenty-four years old, medium build, attractive, slightly underweight. She sits absolutely still except for the slight motion of her mouth talking and smiling.

I ate a whole loaf of bread last night, she said. Butter on every slice. And then . . .

I knew what came next, and I knew her background: wealthy family, domineering mother who constantly trashed Sondra while praising her sister, a mother whom she nonetheless loved greatly and tried to get to love her in return.

I do it because it's the only thing I feel close to, she said. And when I'm doing it, I'm invincible.

It's going to kill you, I said.

You see, I don't believe that . . . because that's my whole life — I've always taken the hard road. I could have had all kinds of money, stability, if I'd just done what my parents wanted. Instead I chose boyfriends who were drug addicts, rapists.

And they treated you badly?

Yes, but I didn't stop loving them just because they beat me. I've always taken chances and survived.

I think I could stop at one hundred pounds, she said, . . . but then I might want eighty.

You'll never be satisfied, I said. When you run out of muscle, it goes for your heart. That's how these people die, you know.

But I can see my body. I can see that fat. It's all over me. It's disgusting. As long as there's anything between my skin and my bones, it's too much. And I know I have to do better.

There was a pause in which I tried to intuit some kind of opening. I offered a metaphor from the movie *Alien*. Imagine that it's a monster someone put inside your body, programmed to kill.

It's all about consequences, isn't it? she said. And I don't believe in consequences. When people tell me all these bad things that can happen, I just smile because I know they're not going to happen to me — mouth moving, body still.

Then she smiled, in case I didn't get the message.

The time for the visit had expired long ago, and we weren't even speaking the same language. I couldn't be sure I was even speaking to her and not the voice that inhabited her.

I had one more angle, a little desperate perhaps, a little risky, but I thought I'd take the chance: I make this effort, I said, because you're worth it.

But the compliment ran off her and lay on the floor as if to mock us both.

In the stillness a window formed through which I could see the hospitalizations coming, the tubes, the forced feedings — hatred rising inside her for those who would dare try to come between her and the one she loves, her accomplishment, her perfection, her art, the alien who speaks her language.

EVENING IN THE
TWO WORLDS

It's what they thought it was, he said. Has Doctor Horton talked to you?

Not yet.

He found implants all over the wall of the abdomen. He's sure it's cancer, though he couldn't find its source.

The call was late at night, from Clifford's son, who had hung around the surgery waiting room long enough to get the news.

Will you be the one to tell him? I'm afraid it's going to tear him apart.

Clifford had come to see me three weeks before — seventy-four, still hard at work as an architect. He had belly pain. We were in the process of finding out why when his stomach blew up like a pumpkin on hormones.

We tapped off some of the fluid. No answers. That led to the operation that had just finished. The pathology report said cancer.

In a wave of regret, I wondered if there might have been some clue I missed. Retrospect is prejudiced by what it already knows. I let it pass.

I knew that tomorrow I would rise early, go in to the hospital over the same commute I always take, speed to the room where Clifford would be recovering from today's surgery, and tell him that what he fears most is true.

My words will not form until they are spoken, reading the twitch of his face, the subtle motions of head and trunk, the silent conversation that will tell me how to deliver the news.

I am as good at this as anyone, and as bad. This conversation, like a blossoming, moved so slowly as to be imperceptible. Yet when remembered, remembered as lightning speed.

I enter the room I have imagined over the last twelve hours. He waits like an architect for his client. I begin with words like *peritoneum*, cells out of place, cells that secrete mucus lined up in clumps.

What kind of cells? he asks.

I choose the word *tumor* — it allows him a small place to hide. New growth, I say. Not the cells of normal organs.

Where do they come from?

We don't know. They're what we call anaplastic, which means they are primitive. They don't look like the tissue they come from.

I have not used the C-word. But he is an architect. He is accustomed to hard data. So *he* says the word.

Is it cancer?

I do not flinch here. My own sorrow, not a part of this, postponed, suspends like smoke over choppy water. I look into his eyes. It's cancer, I say.

He looks away, letting the weight of it catch up with him. You mean I'm going to die.

Behind my eyes I am thinking yes, and probably soon. But I've seen people shrivel and disappear, faced with that reality. The moment will tolerate only truth, but that truth has to contain promise. It's about words, words and the weight they carry.

It depends, I say. It's not the best news, but we can't tell how the cancer will respond by just looking at it. It might surprise us . . .

Message delivered. Ripples moving out. We both know we have reached the end of knowledge. But even now I feel him passing from me. He will be the chemotherapy patient, the surgery patient, the hospice care patient—this whip of the pendulum that swings him to the next landlord, filled more with the present than the past, failing gently before the rush of the future.

And after this meeting that feels like departure, I'll return home to my family, still intact despite everything, and wonder at its fragile perfection—my son toddling off to the living room to gather his favorite books before bedtime, words he lifts like water to his mouth, rushing at life unguarded, not yet aware of the fear that moves as we move, determined to give it his best try.

PART

THREE

WHEN CRAZY GETS SICK

Geraldine is out of her cage again. She called three times on Monday before I could call her back, twice, that I know of, on Tuesday, and now, Wednesday, she, her son, *and* her psychiatrist have all called. It's a bad sign.

I have a stack of papers in my hand. They seem to say that Geraldine is about to go into orbit if I don't call her in the next five minutes, her son wants her transferred to somewhere where she can be watched twenty-four hours a day to see what goes into her body and what comes out of it. And the psychiatrist, as psychiatrists often do when the going gets tough, asserts that it has to be something *medical* that's causing all this.

I have seen this picture before.

I call the son. Can't you just put her in the hospital and watch her a few days, he says.

If there's a good reason to.

But she's in pain . . .

I know that doctors are supposed to be sensitive and understanding, that they are supposed to respond sympathetically to suffering and disease. And especially to the word *pain*. And I do. But she irritates me . . .

. . . well, let me put it this way. We just worked her up for her complaints of abdominal pain and constant nausea for the umpteenth time a couple of months ago. Getting her through the tests was a major undertaking for everybody concerned. She had a thousand questions about the risks of the CT scan, obsessive worries about gagging during endoscopy, strong opinions that damage to the delicate balance of her colonic milieu would occur during colonoscopy . . . she wanted to know ahead of time what we would do if we found this or that, which of course, I could not say . . . and when she got to the table she held us up for long periods of time while she was getting herself in the right state of mind for us to begin sedation. After trying many options and letting her try many, I finally gave the ultimatum: It's right this minute, or I'm going home. At some point we just have to step up to the plate.

All the tests were normal. Which didn't do a lot for her image as a person with a real disease.

Afterward the nurse who would have bet we'd never get the tests completed in the first place wanted to know if I had a degree in psychology. No, I'd just been there before.

So I'm telling the son about this. Everything was normal a little while ago, I say. She's done this several times before, and I know it's confusing because although it looks serious we almost never find anything wrong. The truth is, these blowups always seem to be connected to some major stress in her life.

But the son says that something's got to be wrong.

What's missing from this picture, I wonder. I've told him already about the recent negative workup, that I'd make time to see her tomorrow, and I would make certain everything appropriate was done.

He is unmoved. He says that he's concerned about her taking enemas all the time to keep her bowels moving.

I say that her psychiatric medicines have made her constipated, and if she has to take enemas it's better than having her go crazy.

But she's coming off them, he says, *because* of the constipation.

True. And last I heard, two days ago, she wasn't constipated at all.

But there's the pain and the nausea.

I know, I know. And we have to evaluate that. I will do that. But you have to remember she always has pain and nausea. Ever since the first day I knew her, she's had pain and nausea.

Yeah, but it's worse.

It's always worse and we're always checking into it. But I'm not optimistic we'll find anything.

Well, you remember my father.

I can't recall that I do.

The doctors kept seeing him for his complaints over and over and never found anything. Then he died.

I'm tempted to say we all die. We all see doctors. There may not be a connection between the two. But it would only inflame the situation, and by that admission I know now where he's coming from. This is a cookie from a bad recipe. He has a neurotic mother with a litany of unsubstantiated complaints and the memory of a father who died without a diagnosis. Bad combination. This guy will never be convinced.

And then I realize what has just happened. Responsibility, *ker-plunk,* has just been placed back in the doctor's court. Service ace. No return of serve. The son—because his father died undiagnosed, because he grew up with his mother's pathology and had a blind eye for it—for whatever reason, refuses to take responsibility, refuses to allow that his mother's neurosis can be generating all this whoop-de-do, and chooses to rely instead upon the notion of a doctor's oversight.

Then the psychiatrist comes in the picture: I'm worried there's something serious going on here, he says.

We've been here before.

Yeah, but this is different.

How so?

Much more serious . . . somehow.

She's off her meds. Doesn't that make her out of control?

Sure. But I think—

Look, we're already on it. I've talked to her with a plan and a map two days ago. Her greatest concern was not the pain or the nausea, but just that she would be allowed to talk to me again. I take that as a sign. And don't you feel a bit used here? In any case, we've got the emergency room if she falls apart.

He's not convinced my position in the matter is correct. But neither am I convinced of his. Now we have something in common. And I have the distinct feeling the tennis court has just added one more opponent.

And then Geraldine. Her turn on the phone.

Oh, Doctor Watts. Finally!

What can I do for you, Geraldine?

I haven't eaten in three days. The pain is unbearable. The nausea. Can't you do something?

Are you constipated?

No. I have diarrhea.

How about the psychiatric meds?

They're stopped.

Did the medications I suggested do any good?

None whatsoever. I'm in such incredible misery.

Where is the pain?

All over.

In medical school I was taught that unlocalized pain was not likely to be caused by anything physical. Vague abdominal pain is psychosomatic until proven otherwise.

Where is the pain when it's at its worst?

I can't tell. It's so bad it doesn't even have a location. Why do I have to suffer so?

And I think to myself that these, without a doubt, are the most dangerous patients. They're never really sick. Almost never, and there's the rub. It keeps you guessing. The symptoms they have are for the most part not real. They invoke an inordinate amount of perturbation in their lives. The patients develop a support system that includes medical services that reward symptoms with much longed-for attention, family and friends who are all too eager to sympathize and to place the blame on anything but the one explanation that ties it all together. In short, everything falls in place to encourage and reinforce the problem. And in the middle of all that stands the physician who, frustrated by the hopelessness of it all, is apt to become just cavalier enough as to overlook the one time she really does get sick. And that, ladies and gents, would be a real screwup.

You'll have to come to the emergency room, I say.

Oh, Doctor Watts. The last time I went there I lay around for five hours and they didn't do anything.

Of course they did. They did what they were supposed to do, Geraldine. They examined you, did tests, X-rays. Made sure you were all right. That's the whole point.

But I don't want to go.

Look, Geraldine. If your pain is as real as you say it is, you'd kill for a chance to go.

Will you be in touch?

I always am.

But I don't like ERs.

I don't know anyone who does. But in precisely this situation it's the right thing.

Will you call them?

I already said so.

Is it serious?

What?

Am I going to die?

I can't help thinking that death in the abstract is a great deal scarier than the real thing.

Not yet, I said.

Will you talk to them?

Geraldine, why do I have to tell you five times . . .

And I realized this was Frustration Central breaking through like WLAC-Nashville on a stormy night. If it were still me, I would know better than to believe any objection of mine would change her behavior.

Okay, okay. I'm going, she said. The taxi is waiting outside. Will you call . . . ?

Wednesday afternoon, my day off. I am watering the garden with my twenty-month-old son, Gabriel. My wife comes to the catwalk with my cell. That'll be the ER, I say.

Oh, hi, Doctor Watts. It's Johnny. Let me get Doctor Austin for you.

Dr. Austin comes on. I've got Ger . . .

Geraldine McIntyre.

Yeah, that's right. She's . . . um . . . something.

How does she check out?

Well, her abdominal exam is completely normal. No masses. No tenderness. No abnormal bowel sounds. There's nothing to suggest any pathology down there at all. She's a little dry, probably from the diarrhea and not eating. We thought we'd hydrate her up with a couple of liters of IV fluids. Her labs are normal. No white count. Liver okay. She complains of constant urination, but her urinalysis is normal—no cells to suggest infection, no sugar to make her osmotically diurease. And her blood sugar is okay. I guess we just wanted a little background. How to handle this situation. She's . . . I want to say . . . umm . . . well, how can I say this and be polite?

She's crazy.

Yes, that word will do.

I hate to laugh at her expense, I say. But she's probably the most neurotic person in my practice. She'll disappear for a long time, six months or so, as if she's been distracted by something else, and then she'll show up with a bang and give us thirty calls a week. With the exception of the gallstones we found and took out three years ago, there's never been anything wrong. I didn't want to tell you this in advance so as not to prejudice your workup.

Well, that's kind of what we thought.

I had planned to see her tomorrow, but things sort of fell apart. I apologize, but I sent her to you. Crazy people get sick, too.

Yeah, but not this time.

Gabriel has been very patient with me. Now he holds up his green watering can and asks for a refill. He is naming things and blessing them with little sprinkles: flower, rock, chair. Can, he says. Toe. Toe.

Bless you, Gabriel, I say.

I will call Geraldine tomorrow. I will work her in between patients, lay my hand on her belly, let her, without showing any criticism I might feel, unravel and reravel again. We will sift through her complaints, which she offers like requests for something lost, filtering and weighing, reserving judgment, looking for the one true sign and wishing that somebody, early in her life, had blessed her, too.

JOKE MAN

The police called to say they found my patient in a motel room with sleeping pills and a bottle of vodka. He left a note of apology and a $50 bill for the maid who found him.

Next day a letter arrived. I never lied to you before, Doc, it said. But I did this time. Sorry. I hope you'll forgive me. Inside the letter were two $100 bills. Take your wife out for a nice dinner, he said. Go have a good time.

Charlie the joke man, the button salesman, spent his life collecting jokes for his clients. Long since retired with no place to tell them, he brought them all to me. Stacks and stacks of them. So many I kept the recycling man busy.

Now let's talk about what *I* want to, he had said on his next-to-last visit. I need some advice. When the time comes I don't want to be here . . . if you know what I mean.

I had a good idea, but I wasn't sure. I was always wary of surprises, knowing Charlie.

A friend of mine will get me a gun, but I don't know the right place to point it. And he made a few gestures at his head and face. Does it bother you to talk like this?

I knew the situation: Charlie had terminal lung cancer. And, on top of that, advanced emphysema from all those years on the road partying and drinking and smoking. You give the client what he wants, he always said to me. If they want poker, you start up a game. If they want girls, you get girls. Lungs so bad the surgeons wouldn't touch him.

A gun is a hell of a way to go, I said. Painful. Messy. His expression was like a child's, learning some new constellation in the sky. I leaned over the desk. And think about the person who has to clean it up.

Hadn't thought of that, he said, and took a deep breath. I could hear the sound of cars passing outside the window, the scrape of a bulldozer down the street.

I'm dying, Doc. It's not a major deal. Even the redwoods . . . have to die . . . sometime . . .

He was breathing hard just from the effort of conversation. I sized him up. A couple of weeks, tops.

He paused. And in that pause there was no world outside.

Do you know my history?

I do.

Do you? Do you know the condition I was in twenty years ago — just about dead from all that Crohn's disease stuff? First time I came here, you guys put me in the hospital and changed all my medicines. I should have been dead twenty years ago. I think I got a pretty good deal.

I could feel the unspoken tension of my patients in the outer office, waiting. But I felt no pressure to hurry. This would take as long as it wanted.

Yeah, pretty good, he said. A pretty good deal. And I realized he thought of all those years as a bonus. A gift. To die after he'd cheated death was easy. It was a level of contentment I had to admire.

And that's about it for me, he said. I guess I had better get going. Oh, incidentally, I'm going to need that renewal on my sleeping pills, you remember.

I didn't. And suddenly it dawned on me that this was it. There would be no speeches. No good-byes. He was just going to walk out the door and never come back.

He talked about his computer, the e-mail, how there were so many jokes on the Internet these days *anybody* could be a comedian. I watched him like I was watching a movie with the sound turned off.

And in that moment the room was empty of training and law. There were just the two of us in a quiet place. Even the term *each other* changed its meaning. Here was a friend when only friendship mattered. And there was nothing else in the world but this, this and the river-rush of understanding that deepened between us.

He leaned over the desk, looked hard into my face, and said, How are *you* doing?

The question caught me off guard and I couldn't think of an answer right away. Fine, I said, awkwardly, surprised at the unsteady tone of my voice . . . I'm . . . and then with resolve, knowing it was not an idle question . . . I'm just fine.

That's good, Doc. That's good. Oh . . . did you hear the one about . . .

And I *had* heard this one, and I knew when he turned from the door he was going to tell one of his tasteless, off-color jokes that I would never retell to anyone and five minutes later wouldn't be able to remember . . . and I laughed, I remember I laughed anyway . . .

Thanks for everything, Doc, he said.

And then, I let him go.

THE GIFT OF NOTHING

You are not a doctor, they told us on the first day of medical school. So don't go around acting like one.

Then they told us the story of two young people at a carnival. The girl fainted. The medical student, feeling compelled to act, stepped forward. He mistook her for a cardiac arrest. It was in the days before modern techniques of resuscitation, and with his pocket knife he opened her chest. The patient, a healthy teenager, did not survive.

Authority is dangerous. Coupled with ignorance, it can be lethal. Nor is the problem confined to the occasional medical student. On the Autobahn near Würzburg, Germany, I pulled over to help a Middle Eastern man, sitting with his son beside his overturned Mercedes. The son had a broken arm. I'm a doctor, I said. Thank you, said the man. Would you look at my son's arm?

I was out of my element, an army doctor who ran a dispensary for soldiers and who remembered little about roadside medicine. I recall debating whether to stop in the first place, uncertain what might be required. It made me nervous and cloudy.

Maybe it's not broken, I said, only glancing at it, choosing foolish optimism rather than confessing I wasn't sure what to do, missing the boat rather than declining to act or comment. I think it's broken, the father said. And there was a long silence in which the man and his son were more at ease than I was.

I should have left well enough alone, but I broke the silence: Maybe I could examine your son's arm again.

The father winced as my thumb flipped the floating radius. Like the medical student, I was acting without reason. Maybe it's not broken, I said and left. Only miles down the road did I realize I had not even offered to make a splint.

Ignorance dominates. Wisdom is slow in coming. I'd been sucked into the vortex of apprehension and was paralyzed. It would have been simple to break out of it if I'd just confessed that I didn't know what I was doing.

Action has the appearance of competence. Physicians trained at intervention may lack the courage to do nothing. Yet "nothing" would have saved the young woman and avoided unnecessary pain for the boy at the roadside.

Hippocrates knew about that. *Primum non nocere,* he said. The first rule of medicine, do no harm.

The more I know, the more I feel my ignorance. And the more I want to make peace with that. So I practice doing nothing a lot these days. I'm getting better at it. I told one of my patients I saw it as my job to build a wall between her and her surgeons. A brick wall. After six abdominal surgeries, the devil we know is better than the one behind the next surgery.

I admire decisive action. It can be lifesaving. But I respect inaction in some ways even more. It takes a different kind of courage to withstand the pressure to do something and abide by your limits. So I'm thinking of hanging a sign where I can see it every day. "Okay, so you're a doctor," it might say. "Just don't go around acting like one."

THE GIRL IN THE PAINTING BY VERMEER

Ten o'clock Monday morning and she's waiting for me, my new patient, a woman who looks younger than her thirty-five years. She almost curtsies as she shakes my hand. She wears a light tweed suit that reminds me of Easter Sunday in central Texas.

She has a quick laugh that juts into conversation with surprising speed and at unexpected places, as if she's embarrassed to be speaking out loud. She's a violinist who teaches a large clutch of students and is frequently tired, but blames it on her heavy concert schedule. She's lost weight. No other symptoms. Oh yes, night sweats, drenching. Another doctor found something in her liver, and she wants to know what I think.

In the exam room she reaches down and pats her belly. Do you see it? Do you see my hemablob? Your what? My hemablob. That's the name I gave it. She laughs. And there, out her side, a large bump protrudes, lifting the skin over it like a mound of soil over something buried. Holy cow, I think to myself. That thing's huge. She's looking up at me. Hemablob, I say. It's a great name.

We run a few tests. She's giving a lesson when I call with an update and a plan. She doesn't ask questions, just says, It's a mind boggle.

I schedule a colonoscopy. Two seconds in and I find it. The nurse groans as the lens picks up the unmistakable fleshy, crumbling mass, plastered to the side of the rectum like a fungus gone mad. The room grows quiet, as if we were standing around the embers of a house burned down, kicking the cinders aimlessly.

I look down at her lying on the table. She looks young and perfect, relaxed in a posture of grace like a girl in a painting by Vermeer. But I know her body's ruined, rotting from the inside out.

In recovery I tell her I found it. She says it makes sense. She's been thinking there might have been a little pain, a little bleeding. I'm sorry for the trouble I caused you, she says.

She decides to move back to New London to be close to her friends. I call her at home the next day. Her voice still has that light lift I heard the first time we met. I say I wish I could have found something nicer. She laughs and thanks me for picking up on her crazy way of communicating. I do violin all day, she says. I'm not very good with words.

There came a little silence in which I could not say good luck, because I knew she wasn't going to have any. We stayed on the line awhile, holding on to our silence, letting it run a few saturated seconds . . . then broke the connection as we knew we must.

LUNCH AT THE
STEREOTYPE CAFÉ

Orthopedists are jocks, she said. Football players. That's why they love pain. Then she took a bite from her breadstick.

I remembered my orthopedist twisting my injured knee until I yelped. It's the "Oh Jesus" sign, he had said. When they yell "Oh Jesus," we know we've found the right spot.

Okay, okay, I said, and neurosurgeons are basketball players, thinking of the admissions committee member who looked for that on the applicant's record. Even better if they're All-State, he'd said.

She was ready for me. Psychiatrists need therapy, she said. I said, Pediatricians are short. She laughed. Surgeons are action figures with their power switch stuck in the "on" position, she said, and she brushed a few crumbs from the table.

Marty leans over from the next table. Cardiologists are distant, he said. It's because of their stethoscopes. Gastroenterologists, she said, are intimate. It's because of *their* scopes.

Marty was thinking. I was reaching for ammunition.

Drug reps are good-looking, I said. And they wear short skirts.

Neurologists play chess, she said.

Internists are contemplative and would smoke pipes if it wasn't so bad for them.

Marty leaned over again. That's why they drive surgeons crazy.

I said, Radiologists wear sunglasses and stay indoors.

Fat doctors wear sloppy clothes, she said.

Urologists play with it. Gynecologists . . . We paused and looked around.

Heather came up and leaned over the table. Breast surgeons are mama's boys, she said. Then she winked and walked away.

Everybody was out of breath.

The bill came. We left it for the plastic surgeon.

Lost in Translation

Do you remember the woman I was telling you about with the weight loss and the crazy stools, the one who would call at all hours with her questions of forgetfulness about her medications, the same one who eventually showed up with a bump on her navel?

A story is a story . . . and later a different story. Or maybe it's one story because it has a life where it stops mid-sentence and takes a deep breath. That place. That breath place was where we were . . .

. . . which had opened like an updraft on the smooth surface of the ocean, a place where chaos falls together and seems to make sense. That was the first story. And then . . .

The kids had gone off to the living room to play a little dominoes before homework. So, I'm interested, she said. What happened?

It was the Sister Mary Joseph sign, the abnormal liver enzymes . . . I'd been thinking—no actually, I felt pretty certain it was pancreatic cancer. There is a triad for that diagnosis: weight loss, abdominal pain, depression. She had two out of three and maybe half credit for the third if you consider that a little toxic brain muddling from the metabolites of her cancer might account for her being so bad at telling us things.

My wife made a little rolling sign with her hands, which, in television biz, means, Come on, fella, wrap it up.

The CT scan of her abdomen was normal.

The one you were sure would show some cancerous mass?

No masses, no liver metastasis, no nothing. Clean as a whistle.

And the liver abnormalities?

Went back down.

How do you account for that?

I don't.

And that little Sister Mary whatever-her-name-was sign, the "ditzel"?

Everybody worried about that one. My cancer specialist even agreed. The one strange thing about it was that it was tender. Cancers are not supposed to be painful to the touch. First time I saw it I tried to reduce it back into the abdomen, thinking that if it was a hernia it should go. It didn't. And she said it hurt.

So?

Well, sometimes hernias can be stuck pretty hard, stuffed in there so tight it might feel as firm as a little stone of cancer. It didn't help that it wouldn't slip back in the hole it came from.

How'd you find out?

Things change. She came back and I examined her again, and when she lay down on the table, the little "ditzel" slipped back inside.

To where?

To the empty space under the surface of the abdomen where it lives.

My wife looked at me like she thought I couldn't make up my mind.

Exactly, I thought, then I continued out loud: I saw her primary physician at lunch and told him about the normal CT and the disappearing mass and how that pretty well shot down our suppositions.

I still think she might have a little cancer at the head of the pancreas, he said, one that is leaning on the bile duct just enough to make the liver enzymes go up.

They went away, I told him.

The LFTs?

Yup.

Are you sure?

Sensing his conviction had not been undone, I said we would try to needle the place where the mass was and see if there were any abnormal cells there.

So they found none? My wife was back on the trail.

Well, I sent her over there and the doctor called me in

the middle of the procedure to say there was nothing to needle.

My wife was beginning to look like I was *trying* to confuse her.

I did my best to represent there might be a little bump there because I didn't want to miss the opportunity, but I didn't get anywhere.

So they didn't needle it?

They're very experienced. If they can't find anything to needle, there's probably nothing there.

Good for her, said my wife, then laughed softly. But I guess that's bad too, I mean, not knowing what's going on. I get the feeling things are not adding up.

Bingo.

I paused to remind myself how often the diagnosis serves the doctor's desire to wrap up all disparate problems into one amazing Oslerian pronouncement of wisdom and grace . . . and then, dusting one's hands in self-satisfaction, move on.

Now's the time to recomb the bushes for evidence, I said. Remember how I pointed out she was so happy when all the attention burst forth?

Sure.

Anybody would be, I suppose, but in retrospect it's a small clue. At this point any small clue is a large clue.

What next?

I decided to scan her brain.

What for?

Well, she still could have had some kind of growth up there that accounted for her behavior and a few other things.

Meanwhile, you may recall that I sent her back to the psychiatrist, a decision that I later regretted, thinking she probably had some horrible cancer eating her up from the inside out, and here I was falling into the "it's all in your head" trap.

Seems to me you had plenty of reason.

Probably, and maybe I overreacted to the trap business. Anyway, the psychiatrist put her on Klonopin.

Don't tell me that cured her.

She stopped calling six times a day. And she told me her anxiety went way down.

So at least part of it's psychiatric.

It almost always is. The problem is determining the weight of each part. In this case we had a few red herrings.

Next evening I called my patient to see how everything was going.

Actually, fine, she said.

Fine?

Yeah. I feel pretty good. I've been sleeping through the night. The bowel moments are coming without effort. I'm not as anxious as I was.

Sounds *damn* good to me.

I'd say so. That medicine that the psychiatrist put me

on . . . Why, it's been miraculous. But I've got this . . . seven thirty Monday . . . is that right? . . . test.

Right.

I guess I still need to do that.

Yes, you need to do that. And I was thinking that this case had done so many reversals that if that pattern was any indication of where we were headed, I, for one, didn't want to be off the train.

Okay, well, I guess that's it. Thanks for calling.

I was stunned. She practically hung up on me. She was so difficult to get off the phone before it was as if I'd been talking to someone else.

It *was* someone else, my wife would have said.

So what happened to that lady with the vague feathery stools? It was after dinner. The boys in the living room again, this time turning a Pilates mat into a conveyer belt for their dump truck.

She disappeared from the surface . . .

My wife looked quizzical.

. . . when she got that perfect-for-her-psychosis drug on board.

Stopped calling?

Stopped calling.

Whatever it was about the stools . . . ?

Went away.

Everything better?

Absolutely.

My wife had that look that said that if she could have thought of any more questions to dispel what she was hearing, she would.

And the brain scan came back?

No tumor. No growth. Just a few age-related changes — probably the blood supply waffling down a little.

And that's normal?

Pretty much. I even called her up again. Sounded like she didn't need to talk to me.

So it *was* waving.

Yup.

Waving, *not* drowning.

Waving, not drowning. Or maybe drowning a different way.

And I thought of symptoms rising from her like flags of discontent, the body the last semaphore signal in a language of anguish she could not speak, the body a mirror of the soul's distress.

And I wondered how the body could know to string together sentences that way, sentences that would carry the heavy weight of alarm, as if it understood so well how to get our attention . . .

Waving, she said like an echo.

And after a little adjustment in the brain's sacred chemistry, not even waving.

My wife raised an eyebrow.

Don't worry, I said, and now it was my turn to raise an eyebrow, I'm not letting her out of my sight.

CODGER

We almost hung it up a couple of years ago. The Codger had been my patient since my mentor died and left him to me. Before that, his patient for God knows how long.

The Codger wears a hat with a soiled brim tilted off to one side, walks stooped, partly, I suspect, for effect — he is always muttering about the goddamned doctors and the goddamned secretaries and the goddamned clinic where no one gets any service — and stooped partly, to be fair, because of his rare spinal arthritic disease, often unshaven, looking like he just wandered out of a tree trunk.

I decided I shouldn't take all his goddamns seriously. Besides, I had plenty of stories of my own about the medical system's numerous faults — so we formed, in this manner, a common ground of reckless, humorous, totally irresponsible cynicism.

It was refreshing. Few survived his acerbic knife. He had, as he constantly reminded me, grown up in Brooklyn, a runt of a Jew-boy who was beat up daily by the spics and krauts, and if it wasn't for his older brother's best friend, the full-back from Villanova — a strapping brute built like a boxer, who set him on his knee and sang folk songs, and at other times knocked the blocks off anyone who picked on his little friend — he would never have survived childhood. His brother was no help. He was six years old when I was born, he said, and he's been trying to kill me ever since. Goddamned older brothers. You're one, aren't you? You know how you are.

Misanthrope, he said of himself. But he had his favorites and they were golden. One of them was Ol' Doc Simpson, who diagnosed his Schmorl's disease. Codger would rock his whole stiffened body and slam the desk with his open hand, eyes squinched shut in laughter as he described how Ol' Simpson delivered the news: You're going to live a long time, he said — then he looked up and smiled with gleeful satisfaction — but you're going to suffer a lot.

Peals of laughter. And with the first breath he caught between them: That sorry son of a bitch.

And of Dr. Carbone and his famous response when Codger delivered the taunt from the dermatologist after his rash had disappeared: Well, we've cleared up the problem in our department. Tell Carbone to clear up his.

Carbone was writing in the chart. His eyes flashed over his half-moon glasses, his bald head swayed slightly as if winding up to a detonation of nuclear proportions, and he said, I want you to deliver this message to the dermatologist. There was a slight pause, then Carbone lurched his full body weight into the fist-up-the-ass-to-the-elbow gesture, and Codger cracked up. Cracks up again as he tells the story to me the fifth, or perhaps fifteenth, time.

His visit would take hours if I allowed it. He could randomly land on a small island in the vast archipelago of subjects he knew something about in his colorful life and build an elaborate castle upon it: how he knew Myrna Loy through some friends in Hollywood and went backstage just in time to see her goose a celebrated stage director, then wink and walk away. He knew for sure that P. G. Wodehouse was the most insightful and intelligent writer ever born, and one of the few who showed proper cynicism about the human race. He was convinced of the untrustworthiness of Arabs, the astonishingly low IQs of American presidents . . . I found myself weighing in like a ballast on a hot-air balloon just to keep him in the park.

How's the gastritis? I might say, out of nowhere.

He'd look at me with disdain, realizing what I was doing. The worst, he said. You goddamned doctors . . .

How much Carafate are you taking?

And so it went. Probably less than 10 percent of the visit was spent on medical subjects in an exercise that might loosely be called diagnosis and treatment. But then I figured that about matched the proportion of real disease we were dealing with. The rest? Well, when I finally chased him out of the office with subtle little hints — standing up midsentence from my chair, deflecting with sidelong glances and courteous nods his frantic efforts to marshal a new and compelling subject from thin air, my feet marching their disciplined march to the door . . . little violent spell-breakers to unroot us to the waiting room where other patients, losing their patience over his long visit, were already sending waves of displeasure — when I'd finally almost chased him out, he'd open his Neiman Marcus shopping bag and fill it with samples from my medicine cabinet. You go on, he'd say, waving me away with his hand. I'll just help myself.

When he reached the outer office, he'd settle in a chair opposite my secretary and engage her in conversation for an hour or more. She had learned to listen, or seem to, while answering the phone, renewing prescriptions, filling out referral forms — *seem* to listen, I say, with enough legitimacy to satisfy what was missing from his life. It gave pleasure. He was Solomon at his finest, making pronouncements to an adoring court. It was a cynic's delight.

And I, passing through the outer office, dispensing quickly with three or four patients in the time he remained there, would see him eventually rise, doff his hat, and say, with recognizable sarcasm, Well, David, it's been a little slice of heaven.

I liked that. It had layers to it. I'd say it, too. Even try to beat him to the punch, which never failed to break him into spasms of laughter.

How was he doing? About as well as any old curmudgeon, living alone, never married, an entertaining, playful misanthrope of a guy whose best form of recreation was repartee with his doctors — about as well as could be expected. Maybe better. Which is to say he was still alive, with no serious complications, rare hospitalizations, standing almost upright on the surface of the earth. A man who took too many medications and had ailments that would not kill him but just make him miserable. That well.

But we almost hung it up. One day, in his most acerbic and critical of moods, railing against this and that, he hit upon how I was taking care of him, comparing me to his beloved and charismatic Dr. Carbone, implying that no doctors in the current generation, including myself, knew anything about medicine, or, for that matter, how to be good doctors, familiar territory, when somehow the conversation, without warning, swung full force upon my family. He called my son a muppet-headed little idiot of a child, and I rose out of my chair on the updraft of a fiery wind, and I didn't care about courtesy, or the etiquette of the doctor-patient relationship, or anything else. I stood, pointed my finger hard into the surface of the desk, and said, Criticize me all you want, but one word about my family and your sweet ass is out of here.

I don't think he even knew he'd said it. It was part of the dynamic repartee that had suddenly swelled out of bounds. At that moment his rhythm was thrown, and he stumbled for words, not wishing to recant, yet not wishing to lose his doctor.

It was a shock to him that his words could have that

effect. As if words were vaporous, aromas to be inhaled, particles of humor and gamesmanship.

I didn't care. I was defining my limits. For emphasis I waved my finger. Not my family, I said.

Next visit he brought a picture.

In addition to his profession as a pharmacist, he had a little side business collecting, and sometimes, when lucky, selling a few pieces of art. Most of it looked to me like discards from the low tables of kindergarten, but he saw value in it.

So he brought me a thing of value, a pen-and-ink drawing of his grandfather the rabbi. You can have him, he said. Don't you have a daughter who married one of the tribe? Give it to her. She'll need it, those goddamned conservative Jews.

Weeks later my secretary nabbed me as I was trying to escape the endoscopy unit. It's his niece on the phone, she said. She wants to know if you'll visit him in the convalescent home.

Codger had been found on the floor, beat up perhaps, not clear, somehow crumpled without memory, and had been taken to St. Mary's Hospital, where they determined he had a small subdural hematoma. I went to see him. He was mumbling something about Ohrdruf, not making much sense. He got better, but not well enough to go home. Therefore the extended-care facility that now was the subject of the phone call.

I don't go to convalescent homes, I said, remembering the specific limits of my malpractice insurance.

My secretary knows me well enough to know that my first answer is not always my last. She said nothing.

Okay, I'll talk to her, I said.

We found a place for him, his niece told me. But they won't take him unless a primary-care doctor agrees to see him once in the first seventy-two hours and weekly after that. He's gotta go somewhere. Nobody wants to find him in his bed all bruised up, dried out, and confused.

If I hesitated, I might have been thinking how many times I'd run over the allotted time sitting around listening to his stories, knowing it would be hard to get in and out of there. I might have argued with myself by remembering how my mentor, when he knew he was dying, took me in his arms and said, You're "Big John" now. Take care of my patients for me, will you? I thought of neither. There wasn't time. Somehow I had already promised to go there.

He got better. Remembered more and more.

He moved to a rest home. Very nice. They packed in all his books, even the collection of hardcover *American Heritage*s that took up three shelves. But for some weakness, he was his old self.

Food is terrible here, he said.

It's a Jewish place, I said. What are you talking about?

I got news for you. Bad Jewish cooking is the worst cooking in the world.

I laughed.

Jesus Christ, he said. All this talk about my thinking. You know, the problem with my head is not that I've lost my mind, but I'm seventy-eight years old in two weeks.

I didn't contradict him.

His family had told me that he ate mostly cookies and cheese puffs, that in spite of his ability to charm, he had his moments of blur. I knew that here, under supervision, his medications would be better controlled, he would not be taking four pills instead of one, would not be taking trips to the pharmacy to "supplement" his pain pills with Motrin, Tylenol, and anything else he could get his hands on. It reminded me of the situation with my aunt who swore on a stack of Bibles that the only way they would take her out of her house was feet first. I could respect that. Until I watched her fall — just reach up for a tree branch and fade to the grassy yard, stiff as a bowling pin — as if the earth's center of gravity shifted suddenly and she was the only one affected by it.

I don't know, I said. You look pretty good here.

There was a silence. I resisted the urge to break it. It would have to be his call.

Well, he said. It's time I told you about Ohrdruf.

I settled in for a long spell.

His voice changed here. It became more broken, and he spoke in deliberate tones as if for emphasis, as if assuming the dramatic role the story demanded of him.

I was with the Eighty-ninth Division. We crossed the Rhine. We were first assigned to the cigarette camps. Camp Lucky Strike, set up for the boys to come back home, mostly wounded, ending their tour of duty. They would send them to these camps that were all along the coast, near the Belgian border. We were supposed to land in England when we boarded the boat in Camp Miles Standish, but halfway across they rerouted us to northern France. So there we were. And then Patton's army — he was the farthest into Germany, so when we got stuck in the Bulge, they turned him around to clean up the place and just at that time we were assigned to that division.

From Lucky Strike we crossed the Moselle River, then the Saarland, and joined Patton's army.

I was still with the battalion medical section. We got to the Rhine River, Lorelei, one regiment downriver, one above, one in reserve. We were on the top of that hill. The Germans across the river. Eventually we got over there and the division started pushing inland.

At the same time that we were getting across, the Remagen Bridge was open, so the Germans had to pull back. We were the demarcation between the British and American forces. We followed a course going down and ran into these towns with all of these workers in barracks sleeping on slabs, four or five slabs high. These were Eastern Europeans. We set them free. The medical corps told us not to feed them, you could kill them. We'll come along behind and take care of them, they said. So we freed them and just kept going. General Patton was headed for the Czech border like a house afire.

And there were all these towns. By that time I was the company aid man of B Company. Second Platoon. Marching along, walking ten to fifteen miles a day. The sergeant and lieutenant would go to a meeting to find out the assignments. They announced we would have to get on the road at six a.m. It was April 10, 1945. Two days before Roosevelt died.

I remember we went down a hill, then walked through a wooded area southeast and we came out to a little town that was called Ohrdruf. There is a railroad track running through the town. We get on the track, and as we go through the town we notice that there, where the station house is, a man and a woman are standing. Just standing there. The lieutenant went up to them and asked their names, how many people lived there, and so on. The man started speaking in German. The lieutenant asked if anyone could speak German, so I raised my hand. I had had a little German in college and could understand bits here and there. But I told him that I spoke mostly Yiddish. And the lieutenant said that would be a good language to speak to this prick. He used the word *prick*. I remember that.

So I went up to him speaking English, but then I started trying to speak German, and I realized I was speaking more Yiddish than German. The guy looked at me in horror.

The lieutenant was one of the greatest guys ever. He was a lumberman who used to work the lots up in Washington.

He was the one man who all the boys would follow, because they knew he would expose himself more than the others. As a medical man, walking in the back, you could always tell when the guys in the back would be ready to take off, because they would fart so strong you could smell it. It was bad like you'd never guess. I always tried to get up to the front with the guys who would fire the arms. Willie, the lieutenant would say, the guys at the back are a little nervous. I'm depending on you to quiet them down.

The Germans could always tell where the end of the platoon was because we medics had to wear that red cross. They could see that cross and would know where to direct their fire.

So I was planted back there. We climb the hill. We go down the hill. All the other platoons had their routes. The Germans had been broken by then, so we didn't expect anything a platoon couldn't handle.

So standing there are this man and this woman. Is there anybody who speaks German? So I'm assigned. We go through this for about ten minutes. Meanwhile, the platoon is on the station platform behind us. We can't make out anything of what the German guy is saying. Then finally the wife opens her mouth and says, I speak and understand English.

The lieutenant gives her a dirty look. Why didn't you say something before?

Well, I never want to speak before my husband does.

And the lieutenant says, How sweet of you.

So he asks her what's down the road. We were supposed

to meet the rest of our battalion at a little town, I forget the name, but we asked her because we knew it was down there somewhere.

It's about twenty-nine miles, she said, but it's not this way. It's farther south, close to the border.

Meanwhile, I'm looking at this guy and he's really shaking. Big time. And when she says "farther south" his facial expressions change. He sorta straightens up and has this relieved look on his face. The extreme tension went out of his body. I noticed because I was standing right next to him.

So I took the lieutenant aside and went out to the railroad track and I said, When you asked the woman what's down the road and she told you that, I noticed this guy suddenly relaxed. By now they realized that we weren't going to kill them. They must have been the mayor and his wife. The lieutenant asked me if I thought she was lying.

From the way he's acting, I'm sure of it, I said.

So we decided to ignore her directions and take the road to the town where the company was going to get together. Then all of a sudden this guy starts speaking rapidly in German, his wife translating. We were never Nazis, he said, we were in the underground fighting the Nazis and we were trying to save people . . . and he goes on and on like this for five minutes.

The American standing behind him tells the lieutenant that if this keeps going the man is going to die of a heart attack.

The lieutenant said to the wife, You and this man, you

are a bunch of liars. Everywhere we have gone, *nobody* was a member of the Nazi Party, *nobody* persecuted anybody, and *everybody* was fighting in the resistance.

The woman says, Yes, yes, yes, yes.

Well, who was running the goddamned country, then? You're all liars. If I was a German, you'd all be killed by now. Fortunately, we Americans don't usually go around killing people. But if I find out you're lying, I'll come back up this road and kill you my goddamned self.

He calls up all forty-five guys, and the platoon is off.

Now, all of us in the platoon . . . we were aware of this odor . . . something wrong, something like a skunk smell, something deathly wrong.

We have four scouts out. Two in front, two to the side. We march in column form for about fifteen or twenty minutes and we're walking in a path along the side of the track. The lieutenant leading one column, the sergeant the other. Me bringing up the rear as always.

We pass this town around the bend, then the track straightens out. The two guys come back from ahead and say that they notice a big fence with a wire top running along about two hundred yards, and in the center there is an open gate.

Do you notice any troops? The lieutenant asks.

No troops, but a stack of cordwood about eight feet high with a crazy guy on top jumping up and down. So the lieutenant says we will prepare for a fight. The BAR — that's a Browning automatic rifle — the BAR guys were in front. Firefighting lines extending out on both sides, half with the sergeant, other half with the lieutenant. Twenty-four each side approaching straight on with rifles out, ready to fall to the ground if the fighting breaks out, or go through the fence and spread out on the other side.

We march on, and the stink is practically unbearable by now. Every five minutes we stop and all fall to the ground and get a rest. Then we get up and finally come up to where we can see the fence. There is the entrance to the fence, about seven or eight feet high. The regular fence extends out to the left and the right. The entrance is covered.

From the fence to this cordwood platform is about twenty or thirty feet away, a twenty-square-foot platform with wood on it. With this Polish guy on the top. I had heard Polish all my life and knew he must be a prisoner. So I told the lieutenant that this may just be a Polish survivor.

We walk in, two men at a time, and continue doing that until all of us are in, one turning to the right and the other to the left, bending down with guns out in order to cover in case Germans were there.

Nobody knew about death camps because none of the armies had gotten that far yet. They didn't even know about — what's that big one that begins with *B*?

Buchenwald.

Yeah, that's it. Or Auschwitz, either.

Finally we get the platoon in, and the sergeant and lieutenant approach. The Polish prisoner is beside himself and we're yelling at him, Come down, come down. He goes around to the back and disappears and then about a dozen of us start walking to this platform that looks like wood and that odor is getting worse. Indescribable. You know, I asked Doctor Eisner about it years later. I said that the other army guys can remember that odor, but you know, I cannot remember it. It's lost. Gone. You know, Willie, he said, consider yourself lucky.

So we walked up. Here's this thing about eight feet high. I'm in the middle. I'm about five-five, five-six, and suddenly, from about fifteen feet away, I realize it's not wood. These are nude dead bodies — men, women, and children — and they were all stacked up. And apparently they must have had ladders, and they must have measured them and then put them down according to their size. You could measure it side to side and the whole thing wouldn't be off by an inch.

So I walk up, all five feet five of me, my hand over my nose, and I come up, and my face comes up to, practically kissing distance, to what looked like a three-year-old girl, her face looking out, her body looking out — what was left of it — a three-year-old who had been battered and beaten. That, David, was my first view of the Nazi death camp and what they did to the Jewish people.

He stopped talking. He looked like he was having a hard time breathing. But then he went on.

The barracks extended to the fence on the other side and there were bodies all around, as if something had stopped them in the middle of their work.

We were there for about an hour. We were all picking up bodies and trying to bring them to a place along the ground.

The lieutenant reminded us we were supposed to meet our platoon in one hour. We decided to follow the track and see what we could find.

We got into two columns and went out the gate and I remember I was crying, crying loudly, and I became aware that all the other guys were crying, too. We had about four Jewish guys in the platoon, one of them was in shock. The sergeant walked with him, holding him up.

I didn't pick up anything. We took the Polish prisoner with us. He was babbling all the way. One of the guys was about to give him some food, but the sergeant said to put the food away until we got to some doctors.

Our corporal turned out to be a weak-kneed bastard. He was on the ground in delusions. The sergeant took him in hand.

At twelve o'clock we stopped to eat. Nobody could eat. We didn't think we'd ever eat again.

And you know, I've lost that sense of smell, David. I didn't realize it until later. When I got back the guys were talking about the odor. We rode in the cattle cars, you know. The ones that they used for the prisoners. And we could smell the odor. But it was already fading from me. We never said much. Nobody talked about it until they started publishing reports in the battalion newsletter. Of course, the day after we were there, Bradley, Eisenhower, and Patton showed up at the camp and it was all published back in the States. It wasn't until later we knew the Russian bastards had opened Auschwitz and never told anyone.

And I've been having the nightmares again. TV, radio, you know. But nobody remembers Ohrdruf. And I can't remember the name of that big camp it was part of. I know it begins with a *B*. You see, I've blocked it out. That name. That smell. And you know, odors like that, or anywhere close to it, I can't smell them. I can't smell them at all. It's like they don't exist.

As quick as it started, the story had finished, not wanting acknowledgment or comment—each of us understanding nothing could be added and nothing was needed. Codger and I drifted off to other subjects. Damaged by the past, he'd found revisiting it somehow necessary. Horrible as it was, there was a strange tranquillity after the telling of it. And . . .

. . . we returned comfortably to the mundane, the clerical necessities that are the stuff of long-term relationships: the Vioxx he must take for his joints, the appointment with Dr. Sack, how I don't have Prilosec samples anymore now that it's gone off patent, but I do have Nexium, how he plans to leave this jail cell and go home as soon as he can— we leave alone what we cannot change and tend to what we can—the iron tablets that hurt when he takes them on an empty stomach, the flu shot before winter . . .

. . . and things *are* different now. Transformed mysteriously by what we just went through together. As a doctor I don't have time to spend an hour or two listening to stories. Just sitting in one place that long makes me antsy, feeling like I ought to be doing something else.

Something made me do it this time, made me put aside the telephone, the call schedule, the urge to get home to my family, made me set aside all this long enough to endure the telling. But it was good. I don't know why, but knowing that story changed everything, though it's hard to say how. I could say that now I can see more of the layers behind this complex personality of his, and there was something like bonding, though I hate the word, a connection, perhaps, something secure enough so that when we clash we can still manage to stick together.

Yeah. So he's still hard to tolerate sometimes. Only now it's a game we don't take seriously — all these little rituals we do numbly each day and are so accustomed to now have an undersurface to them, something we feel in our bones but will never talk about again.

I drifted to the door. He did what he always does when I am on my way out, scurried around like a hen scrambling for its chicks, scratching up another topic or two just to keep me there a little longer.

I put a finger in the air . . . but he beat me to it.

David, he said, pausing for dramatic effect. It's been a little slice of heaven.

ABOUT MONEY

I am doing this one for free. My stethoscope glides over the surface of the abdomen like a stone skipping over a flexible sheen of water, listening first, not to disturb the delicate organs huddled and hiding below.

Having now heard their murmurings, rising this time like voices of protest, I feel for masses, organs grown large with struggle against some aberrant force that wishes to disturb the fragile balance of life.

He is eighty-two, the father of one of our hospital staff nurses and the patient of a friend of mine, a cardiologist who called this morning asking me to see him—diabetic, hypertensive, suffering a mild failure of the machine of the heart, contracting, perhaps, against too many hard times, and now suffering from a diarrhea nobody understands. My task is to discover what that's all about.

Then a little mix-up—something attributable, probably,

to language and the propensity of the telephone to misdirect—one hour after I'm off the phone he shows up.

We've got a problem, my receptionist says.

Yes, I say. He wasn't supposed to come *today*.

Not that, she says. He's HMO.

HMO. HMO. Poor bastard. Sick with restrictions. With his current medical problem he even *looks* abused. Frail, unshaven. He has the appearance of someone who has lost weight he could ill afford to lose. Before I hear his voice, I know it will tremble.

I called the bookkeeper and she says we can't see him, my receptionist says. She is being responsible.

I have no hesitation. I have seen this man. I know that we are in this together. Put him in a room, I say, and then I go about finishing what I have to do so I can squeeze him in.

When I enter, it is his wife who speaks. Five times a day, she says. Just like water. Irish brogue, I think. Ten years off the boat.

He looks up at me, puffs a little smile on his pursed lips, then glances back at the spot just above the floor where his eyes have rested since I came into the room, as if the glance he gave took great energy, rising from somewhere near stupor to acknowledge what is moving toward him.

Thank you for seeing us, she says.

I know they've overheard the discussion that sounded like rejection in the making. Now the poverty of his disease shows through, and with it something that looks like gratitude. He is humble, quiet. He reminds me of my father in the last days of his cancer treatments, with his unspoken, undemanding attitude: whatever you can do for me, I'd be most grateful.

To think, my bookkeeper and I had the power to refuse this man.

I say that clearly he needs to be seen, and I'm glad to do what I can.

Now the exam is over. Nothing dramatic. That's good news, I say. But I want a couple of his new medications stopped or changed, a couple of tests done, and if, after the recommendations I will give him, nothing improves, we might need to look at his colon with a scope.

He nods with the kind of supplication so complete that doctors have to be wary not to overdo their ministries.

One step at a time, I say.

Would you do me a favor? his wife asks.

Sure.

Talk to my daughter. She can translate all the difficult words for us. It would mean so much.

She fumbles with the cell phone, nervous that she is taking too much of my time. Comes up with three wrong numbers in her haste. Don't hurry, I say, and I'm struck, almost amused, by this awkward coming together of old-world charm and modern technology.

The daughter comes on the line. I recite the history, what to look for, the tests I plan. I mention the possibility of ischemic bowel disease, since his diabetic arteries may not be bringing enough oxygen to the tissues, but reassure her I want to stick to the simple things first. There is an immediacy of understanding that cuts through the brain's propensity to cloud when dealing with loved ones. Professional. I appreciate that.

We're set but for one thing. If it comes to colonoscopy, I say to the daughter, and by overflow to the parents as well, you probably don't want me to do it. I'd be glad to, and I could even do it without charging you anything, but since I'm not in the HMO anymore, they would make him pay richly for the hospital and facilities fees. The parents look a little disappointed. It could be thousands, I say.

I feel the daughter's nod pushing through the microwaves.

. . . But I'm more than happy to get him started on the right track . . .

The daughter breaks in: We've got an appointment later this week with one of your colleagues who is still in the HMO.

Exactly right. Good.

We are done. Except that if I don't derail the paperwork monster, a lot of low-reimbursement time and effort will be spent, and when it's done, this couple might be out a hunk of valuable change. Nothing about that process appeals to me. I write *no charge* on the front of the chart.

My receptionist will be embarrassed, my bookkeeper angry. They'll have to get over it. We're all supposed to give away our services sometimes. The problem with the HMO is that it makes you feel like you're giving it away all the time. Stifles your generosity. Makes you a different person. And, paradoxically, it takes away a big part of why most of us go into this profession in the first place. I like this arrangement better. I get to make the choice and feel the pleasure.

Yet I am about to lose these people, people I've already become attached to. I want their stories, their language, the little wisdoms that lie in the cracks between opportunity and hardship. It isn't just I who am giving something here. Lying within the exchange of stories and wisdoms they so willingly bring to me, the gifts and trades that make us larger than ourselves, is what elevates what I do from a profession to a calling.

I say good-bye and leave quickly. I want to escape their overly gracious thank-yous and the imbalance of power they suggest. I will call the cardiologist and make him promise to tell me how they are doing . . . just like I'm the doctor who's still following them . . . just like real patients.

Just like family.

IF YOU SAW IT, IT WOULD
LOOK LIKE A TREE BURNING

I have a daughter, she said.

This, in the little pause that comes at the end of the office visit, a stillness in which subjects like the latest sculpting project, the triathlon, the arrogance of politicians, the unexpected and interesting you'd never think to ask about, come forward.

You'd like her, she said. Pretty. Intelligent.

I'm sure I would, I said. And I thought to myself that I have always loved how this moment fears nothing, as if it knows the hard work is done and it's time for what the mind is really thinking.

She's a great scientist. She just got a million-dollar grant to study cancer of the bone marrow and is moving to Switzerland. They put together a lab for her there.

That's great, I said. Quite an accomplishment. Then I raised my eyebrows, or rather, they raised themselves, as if they knew to ask for something more. Silence more than

any question brings out the right stuff. Silence knows what
to ask.

You know, she said, she works in a medical lab but can't
go near a hospital.

What do you mean, can't go near.

She freaks out.

Her mother was puzzling over something, something
that had another side to it perhaps, something she'd not yet
seen, or now was looking at more clearly, like the side of a
face in a certain quality of light.

She was born with a patent ductus arteriosis, you know.

I didn't know, but what I did and did not know was not
the issue. So I just nodded.

And they operated on her when she was two months old.

I folded my stethoscope into my pocket.

Nowadays, I guess they don't even repair those things,
she said. They grow shut or something. Well, they operated
on her, and it was in that famous hospital, you know the
one, where the chief of surgery made the cover of *Time*
magazine . . .

. . . and when they finished they came out and told
us . . .

. . . well, they came out . . .

Her head drooped a little and her fingers occupied
themselves with a piece of lint.

. . . and told us they hadn't used any anesthetic. That's
what they said . . . after the surgery.

My voice was in the tank. She went on.

They said a two-month-old baby doesn't feel pain. They said children who don't *anticipate* pain don't feel pain.

The shock and astonishment was settling in like penetrating oil. I sighed. What part of this tragedy to address first? I paused. When there is no conversation in these little caesuras, I often think of October and imagine briefly that quality of wind that passes through trees . . . how the trees seem to move with it . . . And I don't even remember what I said when she told me her story, but somehow the image of that tree rushed back into my brain, and the wind that moves through it.

My baby cried for three days, she said. All that time she was in restraints so she couldn't tear out the IV lines and stuff. Then she just withdrew. I've never seen anything like it. She wouldn't look at anyone. She wouldn't even look at me.

The piece of lint, squashed and rolled, fell to the floor.

We spent a lot of time with her and she got better. But afterward she would trigger.

What do you mean, trigger?

Something would set her off. Maybe I would pick her up wrong and she would be inconsolable. Or a stethoscope. A stethoscope would make her go through the roof.

The moment was wide and slow. I tried to imagine what the surgeons had been thinking. They could not have believed that a baby doesn't feel anything. Come on; if you pinch a baby, it jumps. And the business about anticipation—you only have to look at infants to know they are absolutely present in this world: They understand what's going on in the room, they sense the slightest change in emotions, they identify their mother and their father and watch their eyes for subtle signals only they understand. They even regulate their heartbeat by imitating what they sense from the parent lying near them. They are wise and intelligent. They just don't have the language to tell us what they're doing.

The infant doesn't feel anything . . . was just a fiction they used to explain themselves.

I thought of my own children, the wonder of their unfolding complexity. And my mind went back to the morning, early, when my three-year-old son, Gabriel, looked up at me from the bathtub and said, Dad?

Yeah?

There are three brains. Did you know that?

No, I didn't. What are they?

There's the volcano brain. Get it? Volcano Brain?

Well, sure, I think so. Then what?

There's the brain in the head, he said, pointing authoritatively to his fingers as if to articulate the list.

I couldn't wait for the next one. Okay, I said. What else?

He paused for a moment, then said, It's the brain in the heart. Didn't you know that?

Exactly, I said. Exactly. Even my three-year-old has a construct for emotion and intelligence in the body.

I remembered the moment Gabriel was born, two months premature, and how, when I saw him lying in his incubator, I could feel compassion and wisdom moving through the room like a blessing.

And I knew what the surgeons had done.

Did she ever get over it? I asked.

Never did. Even now just looking at a bandage — a little Band-Aid — she faints on the sidewalk. Last week she went to have her blood drawn. She had to lie down and cover her head with a towel, and still her legs were shaking so bad I had to give her pressure points.

I pictured a baby on the operating table, four months older than my Gabriel at birth, her chest open, *alive* and *awake*. That baby was aware. That baby knew what was being done to her, and by whom. And that unimaginable experience would mark her at every level of consciousness as long as consciousness exists.

The story was told. My patient brushed her pant leg as if there were other pieces of lint neither of us could see. She was right. I did want to meet this person.

And I wanted to stand with her

                    without saying anything.

And I must have mumbled something like that

    because her mother

                  said she was grateful,

       and then we just stood there awhile and I

could only think of that tree

              with all the wind inside it.

The HMO and
the Renegade in Me

Well, I got this letter from the HMO thanking me for cooperating with the Re-Credentialing Medical Record Review Inspection. I must have dropped my guard. Shame on me to let them sneak in while I wasn't watching.

They said a minimum score of 80 percent was required. And the doctors who scored less than that would be required to submit a "strategy for corrective action" within thirty, and then the little (30) in parentheses like they always do, days.

It bothers me when I hear words like *strategy* and *corrective action*. They're the kinds of words people use when they don't want you to know what they're up to. Strategy. A good strategy, it seems to me, would have been to lock up my charts.

Yes, and one thing more. They said subsequent review would be conducted one — and then the (1) in parentheses again—year later just to see if I'd improved upon myself. Kind of reminds me of Big Brother and all that.

Well now, there *are* certain things I could improve. I'm sure about that. I'm just not sure the HMO and I would agree *which* things.

For instance, they want me to put all the medications the patient is taking in the front of the chart. It's not a bad idea. Except for anybody who changes medications frequently. You get so many scratch-outs and overwrites you can't read a damn thing. So I put that information along with the notes for the most recent visit. That way I know what's what. And *when* it's what. The HMO didn't see it my way, and I got a zero on that one.

And then there's this little matter of the return visit. Doctors always say when we'd like the patient to come back and see us again. You have to follow people up to find out what's going on. Well, I put that information on the front sheet, outside the chart, right where the secretary can see it. No hassle. No mistakes. Been doing it that way without any problems for twenty years.

But the HMO wants me to put it at the bottom of the note that's inside the chart. Never mind that it works better for all concerned to do it my way. Zero on that one, too.

Then they want me to record a physical exam each time the patient comes into the office. I don't do a physical exam each time. It's a waste of time and money. The best policy is to address the problem at hand with your full attention and do your complete physical exams periodically, according to age and necessity. Since the HMO doesn't pay for it, I guess they feel free to request it.

Brings out the renegade in me.

Oh, and I forgot to tell you they said if I don't comply with the demands of this review, they can haul me before a "committee of my peers" and fine me $1,000. For one thing, anybody who would sit on a committee like that isn't any peer of mine.

The letter told me my score was 72.73 percent, which I thought was pretty good considering they didn't even look in the right place for the information. Must have been that 100 percent I scored on all those other little things like blood pressure, physical exam, mammograms, cholesterol, PSA . . .

But the guy in the letter didn't think it was so hot. And didn't show any sense of humor when I called him up and suggested that they should send someone out who knew how to read. I told him in any case I wasn't going to change my charts around for the convenience of the inspector who didn't know how to find things.

He was not amused. He suggested I prepare myself to appear before that "committee of my peers." And I said they were *his* peers, not mine, and if I thought by doing battle with his committee I could make the system work any better . . . well, you know the rest. He stuck to his committee thing and I stuck to my no-committee thing and I tendered my resignation.

Now, you may wonder why all this fuss about charts.

Well, they think they can measure that elusive little butterfly, quality, by looking at the charts. It's true there are things doctors are supposed to be doing to screen for cancer, diabetes, and the like. I agree. And I do that. And I put it in my charts. But quality doesn't reside where you put your return visit or your medication list. I've always thought it had more to do with a thorough knowledge of the craft, compassion, close attention to your patients, and maybe that openness which allows the doctor and the patient to work together. I haven't figured out a way of looking at a chart and measuring that.

Maybe they haven't either.

THE STALKER'S BRIDEGROOM

The treatment isn't working, she said.

Her accent was Eastern European, her hair short-clipped, tapering to the top of her neck like phosphorus to the head of a match. Middle-aged, stony-eyed, she asked about my family and looked at me as if I was to do what was expected, no questions asked. I spoke into the magnet of her gaze. Things aren't great, I said, recent divorce . . . Suddenly I felt strangely inappropriate. I shook it off and turned sharply to the business of the day: which diet to choose, how much fiber to add, which laxative was not habit-forming. She went away. And came back, saying, It isn't working . . . and what was that about your needing company?

I said I didn't. And I hadn't said so. But my protests weren't working. I was off balance, on the defensive without knowing how I got there. She said I hadn't answered her question correctly, but it was all right, she understood what I meant to say.

She bought my book of poetry, quoted lines to me. She came to one of my readings, then wrote to me saying she could tell my eyes were looking for her. I wrote back to say that they weren't and that I wasn't interested in anything but a professional relationship. I told her that if that didn't work for her, she'd have to find another doctor.

She missed her next appointment. Then the gifts started coming: Swedish strudel, a CD of Christmas carols played on a German-Swiss music box, a hand-carved statue of the Virgin Mary. I returned the statue, gave the strudel to my secretary, put the CD on the shelf. Then I sent a message: NO GIFTS.

My home phone rang . . . no voice, no dial tone . . . It rang evenings when I walked in the door, at midnight when I turned out the light, mornings as I walked out the door to go to work. The apartment manager asked if I knew a woman in a dark coat who was hanging around.

I began to imagine tapping at the window, footsteps around the hedge. My mail wrinkled in its box. I asked my secretary to get in touch with her, but the number had been changed. Letters we wrote trying to set things straight came back with no forwarding address.

The situation was out of control. There was no meaning but her meaning, no idea outside the tight kernel of her idea. The look she had given me when she didn't like my answers began to haunt me. I had never seen a look like that. It had rejection and demand mixed into something that was both absolute and powerful. There was no possibility I was going to change this vision of hers, but, more important, there was an almost hypnotic power bearing down on me, requiring the answers she was looking for.

Should I have seen this coming?

Christmas passed. Then Valentine's Day, and the day after a young woman calls and asks, Are you in love with my mother?

Picking myself up off the floor, I ask, Who is your mother?

It's all right if you are, she said. I know these things happen sometimes between a doctor and a patient . . .

A chill ran through me, and it was the chill that answered my question. No way, I said. No, no, no.

Mother said you two were getting married on Valentine's Day. The whole family gathered at the Dominican Chapel — priest, food, music. When you didn't show, she just said maybe there was an emergency or something. She said you were a very busy doctor.

I shrank into my shadow on the wall. A wave of self-doubt splashed over me. Had I, in my personal remorse and isolation, radiated some gamy pheromone that misled her? Let slip a word that became a beacon to a woman looking for entry into a different world?

I played back the recording tape in my mind to hear what I'd said — innocent enough, I thought — but faced with the fallacy of memory and such a muscular delusion to contend with, even to suggest an imperfect life may have revealed too much. I shouldn't have done that. I expected condemnation to land upon me in the next sentence I would hear from this woman I did not know.

It's all right, she said. Same thing happened five years ago with her psychiatrist in Chico. I guess she just put all her dreams on you.

I was too bewildered to speak. Too bewildered to know if this conversation with a young woman who must have briefly thought she was the daughter of my bride-to-be had done what it was supposed to, or if it wanted something more. Was the story over?

It was.

Don't worry, she said. We'll take care of it.

HOSPITAL DU JOUR

George Roberts Hargraves had a black leather brief-
case with a golden buckle. He told us he knew
Steven Spielberg and Billy Graham. He knew the
mayor of Los Angeles, personally. The nurses, house staff,
and the attending surgeon were all impressed.

Mr. Hargraves complained of diarrhea and a pain in his
gut. The emergency room doctors couldn't make up their
minds if something was wrong or not. Friday nights are train
wrecks in the ER. But on the floors, readied for the weekend, it's almost empty. They did the easy thing. They admitted him.

And called for a gastroenterologist. I recommended an
X-ray, a colonoscopy, and a CT scan. Mr. Hargraves informed
us he'd call Senator Feinstein and tell her he'd be out of com-
mission for a while.

A few days passed. George Roberts Hargraves was looking well fed and rosy. All the tests were back and they were

normal. The surgeon said it was time for discharge, but Mr. Hargraves refused to leave. That's when Social Services stepped in.

The social worker came, took one look at the chart, and went straight to his room. It was all there on the first page: no home address, no insurance, no next of kin. Doctors never read that page. Social workers do, but they don't come into the picture until it's almost time to go home. Mr. Hargraves asked her to please close the door.

They had a nice conversation. He'd worked on a movie set in Los Angeles where he picked up the lingo. The brief-case with the golden buckle was stolen. Between soup kitchens and handouts he usually gets by . . .

. . . but if the wind blows, and his hands and feet go brittle in the cold, the welfare check will be gone by the third week of the month. He'll wait for Friday night, then come across town to the emergency room. He knows the best hospitals, with the best kitchens, and who reads the first page, and when . . .

Ritual

I don't miss it a bit, she said.

How do you do that? I asked. I know people who plunge into deep depression after losing part of their body. One patient I know even gave it a name: *Colon remorse*, she said. It took her two years to recover.

Not me, she said. It wasn't working. It's out. I'm better. End of story.

She had come to me five years before, at twenty-three, already suffering from what might best be described as old-age constipation. Her days were marked by draughts and drabs from bottles of laxatives, bulking agents, and enemas, and it all had become intolerable.

Have you taken laxatives all your life? I had asked.

No.

When you were a child, did your parents . . .

Oh, my parents, now there's another story. Mother was in my face. Meticulous attention was paid to bowel movements—color, shape, consistency, how often. She invented an entire vocabulary to describe them. Some stools were called *roses,* others *bombs.* The slender, short ones were *bullets.* Then there were *strands, streams, ribbons, water skitters, envelopes, pellets, upstarts, tra-la-las,* and *matzo balls.* Gas was a *tickle-tease* or a *blossom.* Most important of all, a bodily product had to arrive every morning on schedule, a sum, which observed and contemplated, was noted with the same level of exhilaration as a new baby at a family reunion. Discussions at the dinner table focused on the latest product, and because nothing satisfied like a good movement, laxatives were pushed, overtly, covertly, and obsessively, upon her children.

My patient was remarkably thin but looked as if her body was meant to be that way. She was a little stooped, which made her head cast naturally forward and down so that when it turned side to side, as it often did in conversation, it followed the parabola of a swimmer's head, surfacing to breathe. Her hair was short and black, swept back on the sides, forward on top in a do reminiscent of James Dean. When she smiled, the corners of her mouth turned down instead of up, revealing an orderly row of fine teeth—the kind of expression that could have been taken as either laughter or pain. She had a small tattoo on her right shoulder—a gull or a blackened flower, I could never be sure. She told me the conversations were still going on with her mother.

Talking with my mother is like electroshock therapy, she

said. She hardly finishes saying hello before the interrogation begins: Now, dear, how is that bowel thing doing? You simply must keep up. I heard about this new Swiss herb that is supposed to be wonderful. I will send you some. Don't thank me. It's just another way a mother wants to help her daughter.

I told her if the two of them were waist-deep in quicksand, they'd drown quicker because they wouldn't be able to stop shaking each other about the neck.

She's my mother, she said.

For five years we struggled with her constipation. The standard stuff didn't work at all. So we got creative . . . new stuff, old stuff. I brought out blackstrap molasses. In the end, nothing worked, and we had to admit that the colon was flogged out and lifeless. I told her there was no guarantee surgery would solve the problem, but at least it might keep her out of the hospital awhile. She was up for it.

It would be a hard sell. Few surgeons can bring themselves to take on a case like this. As an internist you learn to play the surgeons by their personalities: some stick to the academic canon, would like to be chief of surgery somewhere, someday, and won't do any operation that is not supported by documented pathology. Others realize life and disease are not always scientific and will spring for the occasional case that requires a more intuitive solution. I knew whom to ask and how to phrase the question.

Ten years later I ran into her on the street. She looked the same, no signs of aging. She asked about my poetry, the

French horn, if my family was happy. She had had a hysterectomy the year before. I didn't ask why. She said she wasn't planning to have children. The madness had to stop somewhere, and it may as well be right here. I thought of organs rising out of her body, offered without regret in some sort of ritualistic sacrifice. I prayed she didn't run out of tissue before the gods were appeased.

For a while I would see her in coffeehouses, writing on small bits of paper—memoirs, I imagined, points of view she might store in a box under her bed, the little sufferings and pleasures she would tell no one, and who could guess, for she looked the same as she always looked, as if nothing at all had been taken from her.

HOME REMEDY

She's a bitch, he said. The word shot from his mouth like bitter spittle and splattered the air. And just in case I hadn't got it the first time, he said it again: She's *really* a bitch.

Dr. Maltiban was my senior by twenty years. He had a long and distinguished career as an ophthalmologist, but unlike most surgeons, he followed his patients closely after surgery was over. He got to know his people and their families very well, and had a strong, almost spiritual, following.

I'd never seen him so worked up. I was doubly astonished because he seemed to be such good personal friends with Sylvia and her family. Yes, he had a temper; yes, he was opinionated, bombastic, and bluntly honest. He was known to ruffle a few feathers. He was a surgeon. But this was over the top.

I had recently inherited primary-care duties for the Lundgren family. Already I had some exposure to Sylvia's patterns. There had been the Keflex issue, the antibiotic I prescribed for her mother's presumed bronchitis — presumed, I say, because the mother was home in bed, ninety-two years old, completely out of touch with the world for the last ten years, unable to eat on her own, fed by a tube through her nose, held suspended like a passenger arrested in the act of boarding the train. Most families would have let her die. She's my mother, Sylvia said. I can't stand by and not do everything for her. So she insisted upon maximum care — and then kept a very close watch to make sure it happened.

Every detail, from the configuration of the foam mattress to the supervision of wound dressings, from ensuring periodic chest X-rays to overseeing the concentration of calcium in her tube formula, was, for her, a ritualistic, passionate, full-time obsession. Had it not been for Sylvia's efforts, I had to confess, her mother would have been dead years ago. Blessed death, some might say; she earned it.

The Keflex issue went like this: Sylvia would begin by asking what should be done about her mother's cough and the slight rise in her temperature that she'd noticed that morning and which, she had learned, contrary to standard medical teachings, meant advancing bronchitis.

If I did not suggest an antibiotic right away she would remind me that her mother required one the last time, that Nana was not accustomed to having fevers of any sort, and that any alteration of her temperature meant trouble. Notwithstanding this illumination, it was a stretch to think she was about to come down with bronchitis. But for Sylvia it was a foregone conclusion. And eventually I would hear myself saying something like, Well, it might be all right to start something.

Which antibiotic, Doctor? What is your judgment? You're the doctor.

I admitted to myself it was, at best, a guessing game. If we guessed wrong, as we did roughly one-third of the time, the fevers would continue until we guessed right or they went away because they didn't mean infection in the first place. Meanwhile, Nana, suffering along without much evidence of suffering, continued in her own way until the status quo was restored, quo being a giggling, pleasant, ancient slip of a lady with bedsores.

How about Keflex? I said. That's worked pretty well in the past.

Do you think so, Doctor? Nailing me to my Keflex cross.

Well, it's a good choice, I said, standing by.

Do you really think so?

And I'm thinking, Okay, now I'm a fixed target with blinking lights.

Don't you remember last time? she said. It took Biaxin to get a response.

I boiled. Well, if that's what you wanted, why didn't you ask for it in the first place? I thought the sentence silently to myself, then, against better judgment, let it escape into the room.

Oh no, Doctor. You are in charge. I respect your decision. Whatever you say.

I was sheepish. Too much rile. Too much energy to the small things. It wasn't supposed to be this fussy.

Biaxin, I said.

Are you sure?

I called the pharmacy. They know me like a neighbor through thin walls. It's me, I said.

Biaxin? he asked.

Okay, so she has this way of pissing people off. Especially El Magnifico Maltiban, who, I could imagine, had little tolerance for the controlling woman, not so well hidden behind the guise of acquiescence. But I'm the family doctor. Pissed off doesn't work.

I talked to Lars, her husband. I know, I know, he said. Whatcha gonna do? I decided that was Scandinavian shorthand for an unsolvable American situation.

Lars brought an apology and a thanks in the form of a bottle. Scandinavian Lingonberry Schnapps. Lovely. Divine. A real painkiller.

And then there was the issue of the feeding tube. It was forever getting clogged—kinked or scuzzed over with bowel jam, resisting all efforts to Roto-Rooter it out.

To do this thing right took an Interventional Radiology team, which meant it had to be done in a rather sophisticated X-ray unit with experienced hands. Had to be the right size tube: not a #13, please—it clogs too quickly.

Those ER docs down at Penngrove—forgive me, Doctor, Sylvia had said. They don't know what they're doing.

I winced. No disrespect, she added, but we always have to do it here in IR.

I called the ambulance, the IR unit, the insurance company, the home-care team . . . Sylvia could work her way through any amount of paperwork, including the unusually efficient roadblock engineered by the insurance companies to stymie the effort. She would work her way through or pester us until we did. So conditioned were we that we started the cascade of calls on the first ring of the phone. My secretary got good at this. Too good. I let her take over—one thing fewer to think about. And as I sit here this day, I'm quite sure there have been tube replacements I know nothing about.

Lingonbery Schnapps was piling up. I gave some to my secretary. She'd earned it.

Then I got this call from the medical supply company. The guy was beyond consolation. It was the hospital bed. Clouds of paperwork came to mind, rising out of my desktop like a slow-developing typhoon.

Nana needed a special bed to avoid bedsores, we all agreed. But the insurance company was unwilling to fund this unless we went to bat with bases loaded. We did that. Reasons were researched and documented why only this and not that bed would do. Over and done. Next chapter. But here was this guy screaming at the other end of the line.

Do you realize we went all the way out there to deliver this @#%$^^ hospital bed and she . . . she @#%$^^ *refused* it! I could feel his saliva on the back of my neck.

Why? I dared to ask.

She said it wasn't the right one . . .

I kept quiet. I visualized Maltiban blowing his top. The image seemed strangely humorous to me.

. . . and she absolutely refuses to try it out.

I know this may be tough, I said. But just give her what she wants.

The man had more sense than to disagree with that.

Lars came to see me. A diminutive man up against Sylvia, a constant smile on his pixielike, northwoods face. I hadn't seen him for some time and it looked to me as if he had lost weight. His smile was frozen, as though he were stiffing it through pain, or worry.

Been having a little bleeding, he said.

How long?

Oh, quite a while. Maybe a year . . . or so.

My God, I thought. Why didn't you tell me? No need to express alarm, I sighed to myself. Maybe we'll be lucky.

We weren't. Big cancer in the cecum, that hiding place in the cupola of the colon with such a lethal spirit.

Surgery. Then chemo. And Lars just melted . . .

Sylvia wept. I never thought I'd lose *him,* she said. Oh, Doctor, you should have seen the funeral. Two hundred fifty people. Everybody loved that man. He was a *great* man . . .

This, over the phone, with Julia Paparatovsky across the desk from me. Julia, by all accounts a schizophrenic, a street person occasionally masquerading as a competent member of society, with whom I'd just spent thirty minutes of a fifteen-minute appointment trying to administer to her lack of money, her helplessness before psychiatrists, the ugliness of her face now that the Bell's palsy made her look like a beggar.

As I hung up the phone, Julia turned the eyes of a slighted child to me: You spoke to her in such comforting and reassuring tones, she said. Why don't you ever talk to me like that?

My face flushed. You don't understand, I blurted. She just lost her husband . . . But I had forgotten who I was talking to.

I've lost people, too, she said.

Right. And I was annoyed at Julia for her narrow, solipsistic vision. My natural impulse would be to explain, to justify . . . but I let it pass. Yet in that impulse I came face-to-face with a strong will to protect and defend my patient. The mirror of Julia's anguish had shown me more affection for Sylvia and her lonely calling than I knew I had.

Could it be that all this time that I had stayed by Sylvia and Nana not primarily out of duty, as I had thought, but out of some deep connection to their passion? Unlikely as it seemed, given all the phone calls and paperwork and differences of style and opinion, I must have recognized something admirable in her enactment of devotion, something that tied me to it, symbolically, calling forth those desires every child has to return love to the mother.

And Julia had made me question one thing more — namely, what the hell was *I* whining about? Whining is so annoying because it is never accurate, hiding, under the flare of complaint, a deeper truth. Sylvia was doing a fabulous job. I just didn't like it because she showed me up being right all the time. One thing for sure, if I got sick, I'd be damn lucky to have someone like her around.

I made quick work of Julia and moved through the rest of my afternoon, a motion that felt a little too much like cutting my way through a forest, some trees falling to this side, some to the other, my rhythms automatic, my thoughts on other places. Julia had neither the inclination nor the capacity to understand Sylvia's predicament, nor had I, once . . .

. . . as now Sylvia spirals inward toward her mother, concentrating even more on every mote of detail, rising before her like continents of danger, isolating her vision to the cracks and chinks of her grand project, the home remedy that belabors her as she belabors it, the weight of loss already felt, watching for the slightest sign of deterioration.

PAIN AND HEROES

Look at him. He doesn't even wince.

It's the ER nurse talking, and she's talking about me. The occasion is a needle about the size of a soda straw passing deliberately, without anesthesia, into my shoulder, the ER doctor leaning on the other end, apologizing.

I'll bet he takes no numbing at the dentist, either, she says.

I know the impact my response will have. It's already been set up: Wow, she says. You're either very brave or very crazy.

I say it's the latter and provide, as excuse, that I don't like going home all numb and floppy. This terse explanation, though incomplete, works better than the lengthy analysis it would take to explain that my scales are just tipped that way.

I don't love pain. But I don't love drugs, either. A colorful allergy history that once closed up my throat has made me a little cautious — well, to be honest, kind of phobic — about the use of medications. I don't take medications. *Any* medications. I took the antibiotic Cipro once, but it was only to make it safe to participate as a donor in an in vitro fertilization the next day. And I took it one little microscopic piece at a time. Apparently I can do meds better if it is for someone I love. I suppose it might be considered pain of a different sort to fear reprisals from taking a drug. Anyway, there are other factors.

This joint, for example, is already beyond the Richter scale for pain. With all due respect for the nurse, a whole cartload of Novocain would have little effect. What is needed is to get the poison out, the little crystals I make like a well-intentioned experiment for a high school science fair on intermediary metabolism gone sour, pseudo-gout they call it, spiky needles that lurk, then strike like a pit bull with white hot teeth. Perhaps that's dramatic. Let's just say I'm motivated. I can take this needle. Its pathway and my pathway to relief are the same.

Pain is a strange fellow. It's modified by the meaning you attach to it. In my case the dentist's chair and the ER gurney are symbols of progress. Not so for my patient, Walter, with the I-can't-remember-how-many back surgeries he's had. He wants drugs. Lots of them. His pain speaks a different language, and it talks to him daily.

Every month he and I have conversations. They're always the same.

My back is the shits, he will say.

I say that I'm sorry. I truly am. But we both know there's not much we can do about it. This is not a casual observation. We've tried everything in the universe including the last four back surgeries, which didn't work. In retrospect we were propelled less by reason than by desperation — always a bad indication for surgery. By now the neurosurgeons turn and run when they see him coming. He's stuck where he is, and he will insist on drugs. He knows his opening line is flawed, but he says it anyway. It makes me think the pain has grown a new function called self-preservation, it just *wants* to be there, mocking us, peering out from behind the spine, saying, *You'll never find me*.

Well, I know where it is. I just can't get there. It's locked somewhere in the automaton-like voice that says *more medications, please*. In fairness to Walter, his is a different situation from mine. I would probably think differently if this pain were a daily partner. And it's not that I don't prescribe analgesics for my patients with pain. I do. It's just that in Walter's case the pain relievers are constantly being outstripped by a faster machine. He doesn't agree, and in the end we negotiate an uneasy peace, fraught with dissatisfaction for us both.

As a child I watched my father deliberately pull his car over to the curb as a very large bee was embedding its stinger into the back of his neck. In the brief, hyperbright window of that moment, he knew that to let himself react to the pain was to damage his family. You might say he modeled a behavior for me, one that would not let pain get the upper hand. I had to admire that.

But I don't like pain, Walter would say.

Now I feel the tissue of my deltoid muscle spreading in advance of the needle on its way to the exquisite membrane of the shoulder joint, where it will electrify as it nicks a narrow window to suck out the poison. This moment is the door stuck on its sill, the crescendo before the blessed release, and I . . . I do not move.

The yellow, viscous fluid with its chemical firebrands fills his syringe. He will shoot in some steroid and, for good measure, a little Novocain, upon which we both agree, and then be out of there. And bless him for that.

The nurse is backing away. I'm impressed, she says.

Don't be, I say. And I know, just like my patient, I'm working hard to avoid what I don't like. The nurse thinks I'm a hero. Maybe. Or maybe just a coward by a different name.

PART

FOUR

AILERONS

I don't know if you can tell, he said. But I used to be quite intelligent.

Cab Cranston is elderly, white-haired, a pleasant old fellow who might have been a shopkeeper or a pharmacist, the kind of good-natured fellow you'd find giving free advice at the corner store. I liked him for that.

They put us all through that testing, you know. They told us we were the cream of the crop. We probably were. Then they made us into killers.

There was a lot wrong with Cab: coronary artery disease, two heart attacks requiring angioplasty and stenting—pushing little plastic tubes through the clogging—just to keep the coronaries open, hypertension, and, to top it off, reflux esophagitis that produced symptoms that were, at times, indistinguishable from those of his heart condition. It made it hard to be sure what was going on.

They can teach anyone how to kill, he was saying. Anyone.

When all the training was done, they even asked us about it. I told them I wanted to kill a bunch of Japs.

His wife, a slight, mellow woman of about seventy, had been watching him quietly and, it seemed, admiringly. At this last statement she turned her head slightly to the side and looked, not at me, but away, and half-laughed, partly, it seemed, out of embarrassment and partly as if to say to no one in particular, He doesn't really mean it.

By this time I had performed several endoscopies on Cab. Always at a time when he had been having a bout with chest pain and the dividing line between his heart and esophageal disease was too blurred to know what was what. Mostly it turned out *not* to be his heart but esophagitis, which gave me an opportunity to give him a little good news. It was easy for us to be on good terms. Today we were assembling the complex puzzle of his interlocking medications.

Japs, he said. But you know what? The bastards sent me the other direction, flying P-51s over Germany. They needed fighter pilots to escort the B-17s on their raids. And by that time the sonsabitches were throwing everything at us. It was almost over and they were fighting like hell. And you can be damn sure it was the fighter planes they came after first. It was our job to stop them because if they got through us they'd shoot down our bombers. You learned real quick that the guy over there was going to kill you for sure, so you might as well kill him first.

I told Cab his talk made me think of my brother, who had been in Vietnam. After whatever it was that went on over there, he was never the same. He was hollowed out, damaged. Wouldn't talk about it.

All those moves the Blue Angels make, he said, they're training moves, the same ones you use when you're killing somebody. The moves become as automatic as breathing, but to beat that bastard you have to outfox him. So when you see him going left, you have to break the habit and go right. Bearing down on him from behind, you have to get in close enough for the bullets to cross, about three hundred yards—and forget the gas tank, hell, we were shooting for the cockpit . . .

When you're in that close, you can see his ailerons start to move. That way you know where he's going before he goes. That's why, when you're that close, they move first left and then go right. To fake you out. If you don't go right first, he'll dive away, come up under you, and rip out your belly.

Cab grimaced, placed the butt of his fist against his chest, and forced a small belch.

You okay? I asked.

He laughed. I don't get too worried about dying from all this medical stuff. I should have been dead a thousand times already.

Cab's chest pain wasn't that easy to diagnose. Frankly, I had the feeling his two embattled organ systems, cardiac and intestinal, were at times playing off each other, each contributing an unpredictable amount to the other, and together to his overall distress. On top of that was the invisible element of the psyche and the role these tensions, carried like a nose cannon, armed and ready all these years, would play. His danger was a cloaked danger, and it seemed to worry me more than it did him.

I reminded him that his medications were important. They might break the cycle of pain and keep him out of the rushing cascade that got him in trouble. My words were orphaned in the air between us. He was military. He would follow my orders whether he thought they were important or not.

You have to go in on him, he said. And when you get close you keep on going, even though you know he's shitting and you see him turning in his cockpit—and all the time he's falling apart, you're pissing and vomiting. That's what it's like. That's what it's like to kill.

He paused a minute. I wasn't sure where we were going next. Or if we *could* go anywhere else. But I knew the story was on automatic pilot.

And when you get him you can't stay there, he said. 'Cause some other son of a bitch will be right on your tail.

His wife was still looking away. Whatever she was thinking, she stayed right with him.

I think my brother probably went through something like that, I said. I guess I'll never know.

When I got back from my first mission, my pants were wet, he said. I didn't know it until I stood up to get out of my plane. My goddamned pants were wet. You're up there sweating and pissing and you don't even know it.

Once I went down. I got hit over France, luckily, in a part

we'd already taken over. When you go down like that, they send you back from the front. If you're in the infantry, you're discharged. But flyboys stay in. And what was a P-51 pilot to do in the States? Sit back on his ass and get fat? Not likely. They sent me out on a C-47, a goddamned troop carrier in the South Pacific.

By now I had finished my treatment plan and we were way over the allotted time for our visit. But something important was issuing forth here.

Our mission was to fly from Okinawa, drop paratroopers in real low, so low they wouldn't be sitting ducks, so low they hit the ground with a hard bump — then fly to China for supplies and ammunition, come back and drop all that stuff on top of the paratroopers, if you could find them . . . then return to pick up more troops . . . and keep going . . . and keep on going . . .

He made a circular motion with his hand.

They briefed us about it. It was perfectly clear to me I was going to die. They said: If you're in the water you put your .45 to the roof of your mouth and pull the trigger. It's a hell of a lot better than what they'll do if they catch you — all those peasants who hate Americans — they'll stretch you out in the sun and skin you fucking alive.

We lined up every day for a week, paratroopers stuffed in the back of the planes and everything, but we didn't take off. Just lined up every goddamned day. The fourth day a telex appeared on the bulletin board: ATOM BOMB DROPPED — AWAITING RESULTS.

What the *hell* was that?

We'd never heard of an atom bomb.

Then, SECOND ATOM BOMB DROPPED — AWAITING RE-SULTS. I know now that if they hadn't dropped that bomb, I wouldn't be here today. Those Japs had been planning for our invasion. They knew it was coming. And they probably knew when. Everything they had was going into defense and it wasn't going to be pretty. We were in for a lot more than shitting in our cockpits.

I would have liked to stay in after the war, but my wife couldn't take it. Years after, I still dreamed about it. During those times, there was a rubber band pulled tight around my chest. I couldn't breathe. Then one night I woke up scream-ing. She asked what was the matter. I think I'm home, I said. I think I'm finally home.

The wife remained silent and looked away. She had gone dutifully where he'd put her, speaking as if she weren't there.

I didn't think about it for a long time, he said. But now, forty-five years later, it pops up now and again. I'll just be washing dishes and I'll think about it. I've even started to dream about it all over again. I don't know what it means. Maybe I'm about to die.

I was silent.

You see, he said, that's why your brother won't talk about it. I wasn't in Vietnam, but I can imagine what went on. Think about it, he said, leaning into the desk. If he talks about it, then he *lives* it. And if he lives it, then when he goes to bed at night, there it is — all over again.

The room was silent.

I've been thinking about it a lot lately, he said. And I only have one regret. I never did get to kill a Jap.

The weight of his story pushed hard against all three of us. For my part, deliberations about adjusting medications, differentiating between heart disease and esophagus disease, were still in my head alongside a silence as loud as the engine on his P-51 Mustang. Even meaning seemed to be displaced, shrunken. Pain was a just check mark on a sheet of paper. Death was just a page to turn.

MOTIVATION

I am sitting on the exam table, waiting for the doctor to come and look at my . . . lesion . . . third time, second recurrence. He will probe it, cut on it, decide whether to ellipse it — lift it like an overripe plum from the surface of the earth and toss it out of the body — or do something else. And I will welcome whatever he does.

And I feel the turn, the departure from procrastination that certain symptoms produce, like that for the dentist, which now shifts like a keel ballast, whipping the boat around. Yes, indeed. I am almost willing to beg to be seen.

It's a wen, *and love the name,* as Raymond Carver says, *but not the thing itself.* And yes, it does rise up late at night and hurt like a cigarette burn, and I feel alone and miserable . . . my body aches, my hair stiffens . . .

I enjoy the practice of medicine, the competent certainty of diagnosis and decision, how it all works together to bring assurance, healing. I know a little bit about that. Still, when it comes to me, I am fueled by the usual suspicions, knowing a little too much about complications, bad outcomes, chemical reactions — the paranoia that knowledge and experience can give a doctor who's not yet had occasion to face it down.

But a few nights of sleepless pain, a rising bump on my leg that, I am told, is not cancer but related to it, and here I am, half-naked on the examining table in the precise position I have looked forward to for two nights now and, yes sir, loving to be here.

Something is about to be dealt with. Just the dealing is almost enough.

The crater in my leg looks at me like a sick eye. Out from under where I have unbandaged it, peeling back the gauze and the tissue debris that comes with it, the pus — *débridement,* now there's a name for it, a beautiful French word for the ugly work of scavengers, which, in this case, means to cut away the dead and dying to make way for the living.

It is the little thing that began as all apparently insignificant things begin, with no announcement of intent, just an unobtrusive bump above my right knee that I thought was acne, or maybe a small abscess. I waited for the opportunity to pick off its top, drain the cavity of its cheesy matter, and be done with it. But it mounded like the crowning of a baby's head at her mother's crotch. Crowned, but not born.

That's when the burning pain shattered what reluctance I might have had to go see a doctor.

You tell me, he had asked his assistant-in-training as they

peered over my leg the first time it was laid out on the table like a modesty set to the side. Keratoacanthoma, was the immediate response from behind eyes trained to apprehend the sine qua non, the characteristic sign.

He told me that some people think it's really a squamous-cell carcinoma that your body is somehow able to deal with. Not malignant. Won't metastasize. But pesky, aggressive. Probably a virus.

He cut it out. Cauterized the base like a lightning storm in the underbrush. Then told me to clean it twice a day.

That was the first time. And I felt better. It felt better. It looked like it was healing for a while, then the burning came back. He cut it again, deeper. Electrocuted it. In a week the pain was back.

Visions of aggressive cells began visiting my dreams. I came to understand why my patients ask the questions they ask: Are you sure about the diagnosis? Is this the best way to go about it? Should we get a plastic surgeon or maybe a second opinion?

Today I will ask questions I already know the answers to. But something about the asking is absolutely necessary.

I look around me at the bandages, the glass jars filled with tongue blades and cotton balls and alcohol swabs, the scalpels and curettes laid out and gleaming like fine silver on a linen cloth.

It feels *good* to be here. Just me and my wound, alone and waiting in the room.

THE PATIENT NAZI

You have not begun to see . . . the trouble . . . I will cause you . . .

She had appeared a month ago, as if arriving from no point of origin—no referral, no telephone call from a doctor—just showed up and spoke of her many, many medical problems, mysterious problems, not clearly diagnosed but precisely articulated: pituitary adenoma, Sjögren's syndrome, Waldenstrom's macroglobulinemia . . . I was fascinated by her deliberate speech, her hard, splashy accent.

She lived alone, had no family, required assistance in order to accomplish her goals. She would need blood tests, X-rays, a scan of some sort, and a colonoscopy. She would need to see the hematologist, Dr. Dalton, whom she described as a troubled man with certain deficiencies but basically a sound doctor. Dr. Dalton did not have an appointment available for three more months and . . . Do you realize, Doctor Watts, that my Waldenstrom's will be hopelessly out of control by then?

She expected me to call personally and arrange this appointment—and soon, very soon.

I seriously do not know, Doctor Watts (and I was conscious how she landed squarely on my name with all her weight as she spoke), how much longer I can hang on.

We ordered laboratory tests, X-rays, scans. There was a plethora of phone calls attached like collateral roots to these seemingly mundane events—time of day, transportation, dietary implications. The usually quiet had raised their voices in a chorus of conditions to be met.

Colonoscopy was scheduled three times. And three times changed. Then, at the last moment, canceled altogether because she, it now appeared, required two days' hospitalization beforehand. I explained that in these days of cost containment it was a request that Medicare would never approve, but that we would help her arrange to stay near the hospital the night before.

Things were moving slowly.

And she was growing impatient. Very impatient.

The calls grew longer, her tone more strident. It seemed that no amount of talking about test results (which were, in fact, normal) could satisfy her. She said I had not called her soon enough. She had been victimized. She wanted copies of her tests. We sent them.

You are in possession, she said, of my laboratory tests of

July 2, and you for two weeks have not called me about the sedimentation rate, which is *twice* the normal value.

Actually, I had. Reassuring her at the same time that this test was not very specific or useful, especially in the elderly, and it generally didn't mean very much. But I assured her we were taking it seriously and would pursue it. I mentioned it could be elevated during infections or as a result of a rheumatologic condition.

It is reprehensible, she said, to have let this information go so long uncommunicated. After all, it could be a sign of serious infection or rheumatologic condition.

I got a call from Patient Relations. They said she had complained about the length of time it took to receive the results of her lab tests.

In that moment — finally — I realized what I was dealing with.

My mind clicked. Suddenly she crossed the plane from just a troublesome, demanding, and worried old lady, the likes of which I have seen before and can usually manage, crossed over to one who intends to do harm.

Sickness brings out the worst in people. It makes us worry excessively. Many of my patients exhibit neurotic behavior. The problems they generate are frustrating, but understandable and manageable. And I have found it worth remembering that the most miserable person in the process is the patient himself. But generally, their basic attitude is that of prayer — an almost desperate pleading for mercy at the hands of illness. Hers was more malignant. She intended to make trouble for me and use trouble as a weapon to get what she wanted. Whatever that was.

I was ready to abandon ship, but as a final effort, I called her, beseeching her to be kinder to my secretaries, who, after all, were only trying their best to help her.

If your secretaries — and she screwed her voice around the word *sec-re-tarie-s,* distorting each syllable until it simmered in nastiness — if your secretaries would come down from their high horse and do something for a change . . .

I did not respond. I requested that if she had problems with the way we were handling her case, to work it out with us. Directly. Not by complaining to Patient Relations, which only served to inflame the situation. I discussed her sedimentation rate with her. Again. That was Friday evening.

By ten o'clock Monday morning she had blown away both my secretaries, one right after another, like ducks at a shooting gallery. They came to me as one, saying they had had it. Incidentally, she wants to talk to you immediately about her sedimentation rate. At noon I called her. She did not answer. By four o'clock I got a call from Patient Relations, a message I picked up on the bus on my way home.

Then I made a mistake. I called her up in anger. I asked what the hell had happened to my request to give my secretaries a little slack, what had become of goodwill in our attempts to solve differences without calling in Patient Relations.

She wound up like a siren beginning its crescendo, Doctor Watts . . . I will tell you once and for all . . .

An image flashed in my head. It was from a movie about a kidnapping, in which, against police advice, the father, over the phone, threatened the kidnapper. Whereupon the kidnapper fired his gun just over the head of the child and then hung up the phone. Just so.

I hit the wall. Time to stop. Past time. She had to go.

Sorry, I said, I have another call.

And I concentrated on the flicker the sunlight made, dropping through tree branches onto our bus motoring down the highway.

I was at my word processor that evening when the telltale message came in, ringing on my message tape like a monotone bell. Doctor Watts . . . you have not begun . . . to see . . .

I was writing the letter. The letter I needed to write without anger or frustration. This must not be an emotional decision but a professional one. My letter would have no effect upon her — I knew this — but it was a teaching exercise for me, laying out from her perspective the areas where we had disappointed her and how we apparently were unable to provide the services she required. It was to be a letter not of rejection but of withdrawal, acknowledging we would not be able to serve her, giving her other options for medical care as I did so. You come away from medical school believing you can serve anyone, can administer to even the most unusual and difficult of patients — an idea that makes you hang in there longer than you should sometimes.

Doctor Watts . . . it . . . is . . . piling . . . up . . .

With each syllable the pitch increased, the volume increased, until the tight tremolo of fury rattled like a bee in a box.

And in the calm that followed, I knew that, like little smoking meteors dropping on the surface of the brand-new earth, the calls and letters would come, from committees, from medical societies, maybe even from a congressman or two, maybe from a lawyer with a glint in his eye, come like a wave of rage that reverberates many times before the echo dies away . . . dies away . . . dies away.

I just needed to step aside.

THE TWO STORIES

You've got an add-on this afternoon, my secretary says. It's your friend Henry. He sounds really sick.

There's always a struggle between the schedule as it is and the schedule as it wants to be. Illness doesn't happen by convenience, I know that, but the day would never finish if we let everybody come in. So there's a little startle that runs through me every time I hear the word *add-on*.

On top of that, it's my last day in the office before leaving on a ten-day combination conference and visit to the grandchildren back East. Everybody seems to know instinctively when I'm about to leave town, and the office goes berserk.

I hold my tongue. Even though I have asked her not to add on unless she clears it with me, something about the tone of her voice tells me he needs to be seen.

He's in the back, she says. He doesn't get up as I enter the room. He's frozen to his chair. His face is ashen and his hand clammy when I shake it. I am thinking anemia, GI bleed. Hemolysis of red cells, maybe.

What's wrong? I ask.

I don't . . . know. Don't know.

Any pain?

No . . . no . . . um, what? . . . oh, no pain.

Bleeding?

What?

Bleeding. Passing blood or dark stool.

Yeah. Yeah, maybe. No. No bleeding. No.

How do you feel?

I feel . . . it's . . . ah . . . it's something . . . aaah . . . ummm . . . what is it?

Holy shit, I think. He can't even complete a sentence.

Seems like you're a little fuzzy, I say.

Yeah. Something's . . . ah . . . not working.

This highly intelligent former president and general manager of a TV station, now head of a worldwide production company, can't finish his thoughts. I'm thinking pneumonia. Oxygen shortage in the brain. Anemia.

I grab the pulse oxymeter and clothespin it to his finger. Ninety-six percent. Not bad. I pop my stethoscope to his chest. Clear. No pneumonia. I think meningitis. Do you have headache? I say.

No.

I ask him to touch his chin to his chest. He does that. No meningitis.

I call his assistant in, the one who brought him here. He's having trouble piecing things together, I say.

Listen, she says. When your boss is lying on the couch with his shirt off in your presence, not able to get up for four hours, you know something's way off. And then, of course, I had to force him to come in.

How did all this start?

He was okay in India last week. He started showing signs of fatigue on the way back. Slept a lot.

I think of wild tropical diseases — malaria, maybe, or blackwater fever, in which the red corpuscles are shattered by the invading organism and the urine darkens with debris. His skin was cool, but fever can be off and on.

Any fever? I ask him.

No.

Black urine?

No.

My mind races to the time he got a urinary tract infection in New York and it disseminated. Ended up in a hospital with blood poisoning — I remember his telephone calls to make sure they were doing everything right. I think of gout, kidney stones. It wasn't pulling together.

I check his belly. Soft. No pain. Nothing unusual.

I call for a wheelchair. I'm going to send you to the emergency room for tests, I say, and I expect we'll hold on to you a few days until we find out what this is.

His assistant wheels in the chair.

Your chariot is waiting, I say.

He laughs and nods.

Encephalitis comes to mind as the assistant wheels him out. I think of my children at home and wash my hands. Twice.

I call the ER to discuss his case with the attending physician. After office hours I go by to see him.

He's sedated, his assistant says. His wife's coming back from Albuquerque late tonight. I can wake him if you want.

No, thanks.

We're just waiting for a bed.

I check the chart. Hematocrit of 12. Good God! That'll do it every time. No wonder he couldn't spark two brain cells together. No oxygen in the stratosphere.

I read on. White cells low. Platelets, too. Bad sign. Some kind of general failure of the bone marrow. Time will sort this out. He's in the right place.

My plane leaves with me on it. A day later I call. He is in isolation. The nurse says they still haven't figured out what's going on. Three days later—same thing.

The day of my return, he is in my office. No information about his hospitalization has come to me yet, but he looks a lot better.

That was quite a deal, he says.

You'll have to tell me what happened. Play like I just set foot on the planet.

Well, they never found the infection, though they think

I had one. He's smiling. Rather than showing remorse, he's the old friend glad to see me, a mood more as if we're about to sit down to discuss a network project we both have great interest in. I can detect no sense of tragedy.

They must have transfused you.

Oh, many times. And my count kept going down, so they had to do it again and again.

What did they *think* it was?

Well, they don't know. They did a bone marrow and there's some kind of problem there. There's a word for it. Myelo . . . umm . . .

Myelophthisic anemia?

Yeah. Yeah, that's it. I think so. Basically it's leukemia.

There's no pause, no hesitation before the word that so many have stumbled over.

Looks like I'm going to get a marrow transplant.

He looks rosy, energetic. Still smiling.

You're taking it very well.

Laughter bursts forth — as if it has been sitting behind a little retaining wall for a long time, as if the moment for laughter has now come and it is happy to be released.

Look, David, I've had a *great* life. I've been everywhere, done everything I wanted to. I've got a wonderful family . . . what more could I want?

There is a little pause in which I wonder about nominating him for the Poster Child of the Society of Great Attitudes. I want all my patients to meet him.

My two brothers have already stepped forward. They said they'd donate for me. If I survive that . . . I guess there's a fifteen percent chance I won't make it through the transplant process . . .

. . . you know, I've known about this large spleen I have for twenty years . . . twenty years before it finally decided to do something. Not too shabby.

You're at peace.

I'm at peace.

We walk out of the office more like golf buddies than like a doctor and his patient with leukemia, more like grateful parishioners, blessed by something invisible.

It was one of those moments that sneaks up on you and elevates you, suddenly, like an unexpected lift in the road. And in that moment I knew I wanted to tell people about this, to write about it. And so I do.

And as I arrive at the point where we walk out of the office, the story is not over yet. The rest hasn't happened. Even so, because writing sometimes has the power to tell what comes next, I can see the difference between what *might* happen and what *should* happen. But this is risky business. The story wants to go in a direction that asks for something more, something daring, something I might otherwise think about. Can I trust the artifice of a story to advise real life? A chill rattles through me that says I had better be sure.

I know that writing has the power to see clearly, to raise possibility, to introduce compassion where the arching momentum of ritual doesn't pause long enough to recognize such opportunities . . . but can it be trusted to direct what hasn't happened yet? The wisdom that reservoirs in stories results from repeated experiments in the life of the real world with all its foibles. Can a story not finished inform a decision not made?

I have decided. It feels right. I will call him up and ask how it is going. He will say, Fine, I sure feel a lot better with all that blood in me. Then I will say, Look, I just want you to know that if anything goes wrong with your brothers as donors, you can put me on the list.

And there will be a pause in our conversation. And something will pass between us that is neither tissue nor spirit. More like flowing waters. And I will remember how I was not able to do anything for my brother when he was dying.

Well, that's how I *thought* it would be. How the story would have written it. It wasn't that way.

I did make the offer: I found him in New Mexico.

You know, I really feel pretty good, he said.

It helps to have a few blood cells in your body.

Yeah, I guess it does. Probably helps a lot of things.

What's happening about the transplant?

I'm weighing being down for two months, he said, putting that up against feeling pretty good right now with transfusions.

I guess you can't be transfused forever.

Yeah, that's what they tell me. But I've got time. I'm thinking about going to Mayo's to see what they have to say.

Always good to have another opinion.

I thought so.

And if you need it, you can put my name on the list.

What?

In case your brothers fall through . . .

There was a pause in which I wondered if he knew what I was talking about. He did. Well, aren't you nice, he said.

Maybe. But you have to consider you might have a violent reaction against all that Texan blood inside you, being from New Mexico and all.

He laughed. Yeah, I might at that. I've got to tell you I can figure out a lot of things, but I can't figure out Texans.

They don't want to be figured out, I said. They're coyotes. As soon as you start to understand them a little bit, they'll change something just to throw you off.

And that was all there was to it. The story had been right on the concept but needed real life to set a few details straight. And there were some surprises. There was none of the fear I anticipated clotting in a ball at the volunteer desk, no experience of spiritual epiphany or mystical brotherhood. Just the secure feeling that when it finished, all was as it should be.

Just that and nothing more.

I write the story and the story writes me. And the story was right. It gave directions to the freeway, even if it took us somewhere we didn't expect. And from here . . . well, everything will play as it wants.

The story and the reality benefited from each other, and

the two stories — the one *in* the life and the one *about* the life, which had touched and mingled, leaving inside each other little tracers, like enzymes of transformation that change ideas and shift outcomes — could now, without ceremony, move us on to the next day.

MALADY MÉNAGE

Because all during the interview the new wife kept interrupting the stepdaughter's recital of symptoms with an almost desperate need to edit minor details and offer her own herbal or spiritual remedies, and because in the elevator I had noticed that the daughter stood very close to the father, nuzzling his upper arm, not minding if her newly formed breast grazed him lightly, what I saw was two women in competition for the same man.

My patient, the daughter, had a simple problem, common to transitional stages of life: heartburn, belching, burning—the hallmarks of reflux esophagitis, except that she also yorked up a little something from each meal—not much, I assumed, because she wasn't losing weight and looked perfectly healthy.

But the usual remedies did nothing. Heavy artillery did nothing: acid suppressors, pro-motility agents, surface-protective agents . . . she just smiled with a look that said, I'm not better, fix me. Simple problems often have complex overtones.

Things weren't adding up. So I did what I often do in such circumstances: go for the objective data. At endoscopy nothing much was found, just a very mild esophagitis. Which left an unaccountable discrepancy between the magnitude of the symptoms and the paucity of findings.

I told her the problem should have resolved by now. Was there anything else I needed to know?

She struck me as keenly intelligent, almost eccentric in her nonconformist adornments — sleeves below her fingertips, well-placed rips in her jeans, nose ring. I was certain if I looked for it I would find a small, tastefully discreet tattoo somewhere on her body.

She looked at me as if I were crazy.

I told her it was my job not to *over*treat patients, and I needed to ask whatever crazy questions might get us to the truth.

She shrugged.

Three months later she was back, her stepmom and dad with her. In desperation, I had given her antibiotics to treat an undocumented infection with the ulcer bacteria. When that did no good, I initiated a trial of a prostaglandin provider to strengthen the lining of the gut, which only gave her diarrhea. She wanted to talk about that surgery I had mentioned for reflux esophagitis.

Whoa! I said.

I wanted to hear her symptoms all over again. The look she gave me said she thought I was suffering from a brain spasm. I asked again.

She said she didn't feel good. It just wasn't right down there.

I said she would have to do better than that. But the closer we got to details, the more she changed the subject or deflected questions, rolling her eyes as if to appear put out by the absurdity of the inquisition.

I persisted.

Her symptom was this bubbling back of a small portion of her food, the part just ingested. An argument ensued with her stepmother as to how significant a problem that was. The daughter shut off discussion by saying, You're mean, and how do you know anyway, since you're never there?

We've had a pretty bad year, said the mother.

I was looking the daughter straight in the eye. We have to be careful here. Illness like this can sometimes be used as ammunition to get at people.

I'm not doing anything.

The mother shifted in her chair, but did not speak.

I'm not saying you are, or that this didn't start out as a real problem and maybe it still is. But sometimes illness works to improve our lives in strange ways, ways we might not know unless we'd seen it happen, ways that if we stumble on, we find out we like and might want to keep around.

Like what?

Like getting attention.

I've got plenty of attention.

But look, here's your stepmother whom you've described as mean, driving you one hundred miles to come and see me, concerned about your welfare, doing extraordinary things for you. Illness can be an equalizer of unequal conditions.

She's not concerned about me.

An image of a dance came to mind, a fast tempo and a beat so seductive the participants lose control, a dance that keeps going even if it means collapse and destruction.

I paused to let the tension drift and fall. My message had been delivered. Impact, who knows? If any effect was rendered by my observations, we would not see evidence of it here in the camp of the enemy.

Listen, I said. Surgery is a serious deal, especially for the young. You never want to do surgery for the wrong reasons. You start *that* ball rolling, and you can wake up at thirty-five with a bunch of organs missing.

But what are you going to do about me?

The hardest thing there is to do. Nothing. Actually, it's a little more than that. Support. Observation. I think in a couple of years when you leave home this thing will go away. Sometimes the best I can do for people is to keep them from getting hurt long enough to let natural processes take over. Think about it.

I take it as a good sign that I haven't seen her. I hope that the malady has been split into its parts, and in parts, can do no harm. I could be wrong. She may have another doctor by now, may have started her litany of surgeries, may have hard feelings for a doctor who cut into her tight world, cut in as an uninvited partner at a private dance, an interloper whose only recommendation was to slow down the music.

PROTECTION

Somebody's trying to kill me, he said.

I hadn't seen Stanley for years — change of jobs, maybe his insurance — there were no road signs to tell me why.

Times like this I try to take up the weaving at the spot we left in the nap years ago. But this reentry was going to be tangled.

What are you talking about? I asked.

There had been a death at work, someone young, physically fit — a drowning, maybe, a disappearance — details were vague. Death is never vague, I thought. There's more to it.

The woman who disappeared was a key figure in some kind of investigation, some alleged wrongdoing. It was sounding like a story for Elliot Ness.

People started getting phone calls, threats. There was a fight at work — someone showed up with seven stitches, a few puffy hematomas fading to yellow in the tense weeks that followed. The place started looking seedy. Somehow he was in this, or thought he was. He started getting telephone calls in the middle of the night.

It's my arthritis, he said. It feels like someone took a cattle prod to my joints and forgot to turn it off. I looked. There were the telltale signs of inflammation: *tumor, rubor, calor, dolor* — swelling, redness, heat, pain. The knee joint was out like a burl on a redwood tree. Nasty, I said. What are you doing for this?

We talked about management of rheumatoid arthritis, the drugs that reduce pain and swelling and side effects: gastritis, bleeding, et cetera. I assumed that under this much stress he would be susceptible to side effects. I was feeling at home in the discussion of pathophysiology and treatment, not relishing a return to the drama.

But he kept going back to it. Any lull was the needle drop for the broken record.

I don't want to appear insensitive, I said, but I don't know a thing about the trouble you're in. Maybe you need a lawyer, or the police . . .

I wrote some prescriptions, made a few recommendations, drew blood for chemistry and hematology, and scheduled a return visit in two weeks.

He came back, no better. I told him he needed to resolve his life before his body was going to cooperate. He said he had a lawyer and was going after the bastards . . . things were getting tight.

I began to realize this *was* his life. He thought about it

night and day, got up in the middle of the night to take down notes, replayed it in his mind a thousand times, one violent scenario after another. Now he was drawing me into it.

Can you do something? Talk to the police or something?

My two minds squared off. Give help. Keep yourself and your family out of the way of crime.

Stanley, I said, I'm a doctor. If I had the training and experience, it might be different. I can say what I know to say: There is a relationship between your stress and this flare-up. After that it's a legal matter, or a police matter. Best if I don't know details.

The arthritis smoldered like an iguana in an angry sun. I adjusted medications, told him to get psychiatric help, try to separate himself from this freight train or it would drag him deep into the next county. He wasn't listening.

He came back saying his lawyer had advised him to drop the case and move out of town. Stanley was certain they'd bought the lawyer off. He was having nightmares. The arthritis was worse. I felt as if I were listening to a man with a brain tumor whose tumor was doing all his talking.

Why are you going so far with this? I asked.

I have all these bills to pay, and I need to get on with my life. But I have to say I'm sick of talking to lawyers. Everybody knows I'm a wreck. My cat jumps off my lap when the telephone rings.

I have no way of knowing if what you say is true. But if you are in grave danger, you have to remember, it's just money.

His girlfriend had accompanied him that day. She broke into tears, saying something about obsession.

He told her he would drop the lawsuit. Everything appeared to be settled. And if it were a Hollywood script, it would end right here: protagonist chooses not the heroism of self-sacrifice but the valor of a peaceable life.

Next day there was a lawyer's brief on my desk. It suggested how my testimony might help once they got to court. It's clicked over, I said to no one in particular.

I was in the dark. Beyond what I knew about his medical condition, there were parts of this large fiction I couldn't see, shapes that moved like bats in a dangerous cave. How could I know the border between the real and the imagined, between safety and danger, between the external theater of images and the real story? I had struggled not to be out of my element, but somehow I was, an unwilling a player in someone else's dream, a direction without plan or denouement, knowing no more than the demand in front of me, reading no message more clearly than the expression on the face of the next request.

I was never called to testify. For all I know, the matter never went to court. Stanley disappeared from my practice just as he had before, without warning or explanation. I worried about his safety, armed only with his memory and his notepad against a danger too unimaginable to name, too invasive to turn him loose.

A year later, driving home, I caught a glimpse of him standing at a bus stop. He looked good, happy even. I was shocked to see him, more shocked to see him this way, so different from the projections of his future he had conjured up for me. This image made the heft of his story waffle and lift away with a sigh. He could still be in some sort of trouble, I supposed, but it didn't appear that way. I guess I was just glad to see him alive, alive and spirited, standing patiently, notepad in hand, waiting for the next bus to come.

CONSULTATION

I'm seventy-five and I have severe heart disease, he said.

He's a doctor, so I assume he knows what he's talking about. He's been sent here by his primary physician to have a colonoscopy. We've already had that discussion with his wife, and I know by his interjections he is not enthusiastic about the idea in general. She has decided on good grounds to schedule hers. Now it's his turn to step up to the plate.

Already I know that part of the reason they've come is to be sure I don't have two heads or something—that I'm human, not likely to duplicate unpleasant experiences they've had at the hands of others. She flashed with anger at her gastroenterologist of six years for losing her previous colonoscopy report and not seeming to care. But she has decided. I must have passed the test.

Now it's her husband's turn. I'm not sure I want to do this, he says.

Several times during his wife's interview he had said, I don't think you should do it. Decisions, especially wrong ones, love company.

If she came to test my professionalism, he was here for something else.

I studied him for a moment. He was going to be tough.

So you don't want go out at colonoscopy? I said.

He laughed, but a little fleck of fear was in his eyes. Good, I thought, a myth exposed, often dispelled.

Oh, I'm not worried about that, he said. I'll survive colonoscopy.

I was still watching him, closely.

He paused, considering whether to say the next thing, as if to assess whether he and the room could take it.

I'm not interested in finding a tumor that already exists. Then he paused and turned to his wife. Though just saying that makes me more inclined to go ahead.

So that was it. He didn't want life ruined by the knowledge of something fatal, something he could do nothing about. Okay with me, I thought, as long as the tumor is already terminal. But what about the ones you can catch in time? In front of us was the door with the words "Ideas of My Death" written on it. We had to open that thing up to get beyond it.

How long are you planning to live? I asked.

He squirmed, then laughed the kind of laugh that realizes at the heart of his discomfort lies a critical issue.

Well, as long as I can, he said.

I should hope so, I said. And who knows, you could go on for another fifteen years. But if you're already planning to die of heart disease five years from now, well, then I guess you don't need a colonoscopy.

I don't know, he said, turning to his wife. Do you think you could put up with me another fifteen years?

Better if you don't have colon cancer, she said.

He was on the spot. His wife was looking at him as though hearing something she'd never heard before.

This goes back a bit, he said, and shifted in his chair.

When the cardiac surgeon finished my coronary bypass and came out to talk to my family, the first thing he said was, I'm sorry. I'd hoped for another ten years. It was a horrible thing to say. Affected my whole family . . . for years. That was twelve . . .

Thirteen, his wife said.

. . . thirteen years ago this fall.

Well, now that you've proved him wrong, I said, no need to continue living under his spell.

Maybe this is all crazy, he said.

No, it makes sense, I said. It seems to me like you're just trying to determine the intersection of some pretty unpredictable lines. Okay by me. Just don't underestimate your trajectory. How *is* your heart, anyway?

Good. It was his wife that answered.

Well, the myocardium is okay, he said. I wouldn't say the same for the coronaries.

She has more faith than you do, I said.

Probably.

Have you had any trouble since the surgery?

No.

And I tried to imagine what it must be like for thirteen years in a row to think that you're not going to make it to your next birthday. If I believed that, I wouldn't want colonoscopy, either.

He wanted to know what kind of preparation, what I used for sedation, my track record, after which he looked around the room as though checking his whereabouts, then said, Yup, I think I'll do it.

Too easy, I thought. This is a complex man. True, we can often think better when someone else is listening, but there's a distinction to be made between cooperative deliberation and persuasion. I was afraid we might have done the latter.

Take your time, I said, think it over.

On the way to the front desk we talked of other things: He was a psychiatrist, didn't I feel that gastroenterology was laced with a strong dash of psychology, what days did I do colonoscopies, how much he enjoyed his practice, loved to play golf . . .

They chatted with my receptionist for a while, then left. When I stopped by the desk and looked, there was a place in my book with his name written on it.

THE THIRD SATISFACTION

The first time I saw her she was naked, stretched out on a chaise longue, sunbathing in the fourth-floor solarium of the University Hospital. I was a young doctor then, and I was startled not only for stumbling upon her in the buff, but for the unaccustomed feelings, a strange mixture of curiosity and embarrassment, that rose in me.

What's the big deal? she said. Isn't this a hospital?

She wasn't my patient, but on weekends I took calls for an older doctor who, tirelessly it seemed to me, looked after her.

What's your name? she asked.

I don't give my name to naked people.

Oh, all right, she said. You'd think by now everyone around here would have seen it all.

Doctor Watts, I said, as she slipped on her blouse.

I can see that on your name tag. I mean what's your *name?*

David. David Watts.

Okay, David, she said. So is this the best excuse they have for doctors around here?

She didn't love house staff or young faculty, so any peace I was to negotiate was to be a fragile one — mostly, I noticed, on her terms. But then, I only had to take care of her on weekends.

Now, J.B. forgot — he's a dear, but he's a little preoccupied sometimes — J.B. forgot to up my Dilaudid suppositories to three times a day instead of two.

I must have had a blank look on my face.

I'm in a lot of pain from my Crohn's.

I looked her over: sunglasses, matador's hat, plunging (recently buttoned) neckline, aroma of Paris Nights, headphones . . . It didn't look like pain to me.

And I remembered only too well J.B.'s general view on narcotic prescriptions on the weekend: Anybody who can't get their act together to arrange for pain medications during the week is up to something.

Maybe I'll call him up, I said.

She rolled her eyes. Now, David, don't tell me we're going to start what could be a perfectly fine relationship on such a sour note.

It's a matter of clarity.

Okay, okay. Call him up. But do me a little favor and increase my prescription *before* you call him. I'm just a little tired of waiting.

I didn't do either. Well, at least that's how I like to remember it. I was so easily intimidated in those days, I probably went right down the hall and wrote the order just as she instructed, not fully understanding the clinch I felt inside, like the ones I felt as a child when I did something only because somebody expected it of me.

In any case, by the next morning the hot issue of the previous day didn't exist. It had never existed, and any discussion of medications had been replaced by her growing perception that she had known me in a previous life. Wasn't it I who, when she lived near Aransas Pass, came to her house as the spirit of a dead pirate looking for his gold?

If I'd found it I wouldn't be *here,* I said.

Oh, it was you, all right. But the gold was under the floorboard, and I woke up just in time to shoo you back to your Spanish galleon. Don't you remember?

I said nothing.

You remember. You just don't remember you remember.

You — and I paused for effect — are a wild woman.

You jes' have to get to know me, she sassed.

Which is, of course, exactly what happened. My mentor died and left Rochelle to me in his will — well, almost like that. Just before he died he put his arm around my shoulder and said, You're "Big John" now. Can I depend on you to take care of my people?

That was just a few minutes after Rochelle had left his hospital room in a wild state of hysteria. What do you mean, dying like this? she screamed. Of all the heartless — Words sputtered at the prospect of finishing her sentence. How do you expect me to survive if you're not around?

Ten past midnight, and a call comes in on my cell phone. It is a few weeks later and I am on a short vacation with my family to Lake Tahoe, where I've just arrived or I would be asleep by now.

David, why did you change my medication?

It's Rochelle, in the hospital back in San Francisco. She's pissed off because she only gets her Dilaudid suppositories twice a day. She has my cell-phone number because I gave it to her. Saves time, I reasoned, and patients get to feel more connected to their doctor. Most people call *less* often if they know they have my number. It's like the pill in the medicine cabinet you don't take that keeps you well. In Rochelle's case it was a bad idea.

By now I had almost grown accustomed to the black negligees, the low-cut necklines, perfume that blistered your nostrils, and the attitude of excessive familiarity she took with her doctors — seductive, the social worker called it. Exhibitionism, I thought. It didn't seem to have much to do with sex.

When she was not wearing her bedroom attire, she wore a jumpsuit and a baseball cap with the words "Spoiled Rotten" across the front. She was accustomed to getting her way, and even her doctors finally just gave up and did pretty much what she wanted, took calls at all hours, gave her drugs. Persuasive, charismatic, forceful — she was one of those electric people who change the ecology of the room she's in.

I wanted to be responsible. To say that was going to be difficult was an understatement. I wasn't so sure she was as sick as she thought she was. But her disease was wacky, the kind that's unpredictable both in how it presents itself and how much she uses it to upset the applecart of equilibrium. She'd already been whittled on several times, and her belly was, in the words of one of my professors, a home run — a scar in every quadrant. Looking back on it, I wasn't sure if they'd cut her for disease or for symptoms.

I think you're addicted, I said.

She scoffed and rolled her eyes. Don't you know anything? Don't you know how I left the hospital and stopped drugs just like that? She snapped her fingers. Could I do that if I was addicted? No way!

We wandered off to something we could agree upon: the insanity of the current political administration, the inane clerks who have no business controlling medical decisions over the phone . . . She was talkative, gregarious, entertaining.

You should be a talk show host, I said.

Now, David, if you can say that, you don't know my life. How could I do that and have this disease?

President Eisenhower had this disease, other people . . .

He didn't have *my* disease, that's all I can say about it.

It's a waste. You've got talent.

I'm doing just fine, thank you. I'm hanging. That's about all I can do is hang. You've got to hang to stay around in this world.

She paused and glared at me. Okay. So you don't believe my pain.

I believe it. I'm just not sure I can take it away.

Then let me get this straight. You've just decided to *let the patient suffer.*

I anticipated the last four words, and we said them together with a syrupy, musical ritardando accompanied by a little sarcastic lilting crescendo. That's cute, I said.

I'm not being cute.

Yes, you are, real cute. And I shriveled inside. Damn it! I'd let myself be drawn into an unprofessional argument. She'd made me mad, and mad defeated me.

I wrote the blankety-blank prescriptions.

In the middle of the night I woke up and realized that what frustrated me so much was that my efforts to take care of her had earned not a farthing of thanks. Her self-centeredness was immaculate and could shatter glass. No need for appreciation when service is the going currency. That meant the anger she provoked in me came from expecting . . . what? Maybe it was gratitude that was missing, gratitude that gave me a feeling of satisfaction. Right then, I learned something about myself.

And I changed the plan. I was going to have to get over the gratitude thing. Just do my job the way I was supposed to, and let that be my satisfaction. At least I had control over that. With this attitude I would do a better job.

And now Rochelle wanted to be in the hospital again.

I don't think I'm going to live much longer and I don't want to be reminded of it, she said. But I'm not doing well and I think about three weeks of in-the-hospital hyper-alimentation would do it, you know, a little food in my arm.

Do what?

Put me back on my feet again.

You know it's not customary to hospitalize patients just for hyperalimentation. The Utilization Review Committee would be on my back.

I'm sick. I'm losing weight. I'm in pain. What does a girl have to do to get in the hospital these days?

I could see it in my mind. It wasn't difficult to assemble the images out of past experience: Rochelle smoking in her hospital room and trying to cover it up with incense, walking up and down the corridor, dragging her IV pole behind her, wearing black negligees that plunged all the way to her belly button, demanding drugs, drugs, and more drugs.

By now she had already "failed" our attempts to give her intravenous nourishment at home. She was hard to find. Wouldn't be there when the nurses came to start the infusion. Kept moving back and forth between her parents' house in Berkeley and her apartment in San Francisco. When we finally did get it started, the infusion line kept inexplicably falling out or getting dislodged. And the paraphernalia, she said, disturbed her spirit.

We should be able to do this at home, I said.

I don't love going into the hospital, she said. I don't know if you know this, but I'm claustrophobic. I have to tell myself I'm not there in order to survive those small hospital rooms. Whatever is happening, happens to my body but not to me. That's why I dress the way I do, put on makeup, and burn incense. I play games. It's just survival.

We made a contract. No more pain medications than she is now taking. No smoking in the room. Then I called the admitting resident.

I told her about Rochelle's Crohn's, her surgeries, her short-gut syndrome, the recent weight loss, my attempts to build her up with home IV nourishment, the six-pound weight loss in one week, and the crunch I found myself in, needing to bring her in, believing she may have provoked her own weight loss. I told her I wanted to evaluate the ability of the bowel to absorb, to move toward outpatient care as soon as possible and manage her pain. Now the bomb-drop: She's difficult, I say. Has a problem with pain meds, demanding. I told her about the provisions of our contract. She doesn't love interns and students and will try to fire them from her case. One thing more: Because of the compensatory hypertrophy of the small bowel, it can at times appear to be dilated as if from obstruction. She's not obstructed, and her Crohn's has not, by my estimation, been active for some time. She believes she will die soon, but she is the only one who thinks so.

The resident took it all pretty well. It was a frank beginning. Everyone was on the same page.

At 3:00 p.m. my secretary interrupted me to say that Rochelle had arrived on the hospital ward and was demanding her Dilaudid suppository *right now*. I said nothing and returned to my work.

After hours I made rounds. Rochelle was as happy as a child with a new toy. I figured she'd gotten her suppository, but when I checked the chart I saw she hadn't.

Next day she refused the hyperalimentation line. That's the *reason* for this hospitalization, I said.

I don't want that thing hanging out of me, she said.

Then the chief of Interventional Radiology made it known he didn't feel she was a candidate anyway, because of her attitude.

That night I got a call from her mother. She said Rochelle had had a hard day.

So have I, I said.

Couldn't you just give her something to make her happy?

No.

Why not?

We have a contract.

I know about that, but she's in pain. At the sound of the word, the hairs on the back of my neck bristled. I thought of the millions of freeloaders riding stowaway on the heft of that word.

Why are you doing this? I asked.

What?

Calling me up. Asking for more pain medications for your daughter.

Why, she's my daughter. And I want her to be comfortable. Can't you just give her something?

I can't because — and I thought a moment, then decided to be blunt — because she's probably addicted to narcotics, and the pain may be her avenue to get them.

Oh! I didn't know that . . . But can't you just give her something?

It took my breath away. I was in the interior beehive, the breeding ground for rituals that spread like instinct down through the generations. It was all beginning to make sense.

The resident called and said she thought Rochelle was doing drugs in the hospital. The nurses found her stuporous, and she'd been asking for rubber bands.

We need to do a drug screen, I said.

Nutritionally she's doing fine, the resident said, in positive nitrogen balance and the fat absorption is completely normal.

She didn't need hyperalimentation in the first place.

Exactly. And I don't think she'll be properly prepped for her colonoscopy tomorrow. The nurses walked in at midnight, and three-quarters of her bowel prep was still there. Eight minutes later it was gone.

Dumped it.

She dumped it.

I went to the ward, but I couldn't find her chart. The ward clerk was hiding it under the desk because Rochelle had been altering the doctor's notes. Portions of my writing had been blackened over with a broad dark swipe. I remembered what it was she'd marked out: suicide attempt last fall, three days in a psychiatric institute.

A little misunderstanding, Rochelle said.

Any attempt is a serious attempt, I had said.

You have altered a legal document, the nurse said.

That afternoon the drug screen came back positive for cocaine and cocaine metabolites. The picture was complete:

no malabsorption, *no* Crohn's flare-up, *no* obstruction, *no* need for hyperalimentation . . . and, by God, *no* more narcotic prescriptions from me.

On the way out of the hospital she dropped by the office for her Dilaudid. I told her I thought she needed help with her narcotic problem.

Now, David, I make the mistake of telling you I did cocaine once around Christmastime, and now you think I'm hooked. I can't say *anything* around you.

Your drug test was positive for cocaine. It means you've had it in the last few hours.

Positive?

Yes.

Are you sure it was me?

Yes.

They probably mixed up the specimens.

Not likely. Besides, it matches with you being so gorked-out all the time.

So that's how it is, huh? I see. Well, I can look you in the eye and say I didn't do it.

I leaned over the table and looked at her up close. Yes, you can look me in the eye and say that you didn't do it. And that's just the problem.

She turned away, screwed up her mouth, and waved her hand as if throwing something out of her ear. Well, you can choose to believe a computer, or you can choose to believe me.

You've got to get hold of this drug thing, I said. Why don't you enter a rehab unit?

You know I can't do that. Those fools don't know how to tie their own shoes.

The choices are getting fewer, I said.

She left. And I felt relieved. But I argued with myself. Couldn't it be said that if someone wanted to live out her life on drugs, it was really up to her? Maybe the way my predecessor did it, providing her with her prescriptions, was a way of being present in case he needed to dig her out of the hard spots later on. Maybe that was another way of interpreting the phrase *giving care*.

No, said the ward nurse. She's got that attitude that says "the whole world owes me." And you know what? I'm sorry if she has to do drugs so as not to face her miserable life, but she doesn't have to drag you into it.

Rochelle fired me. We've been together a long time, David, she said. It's time we moved on. And, by the way, you probably needed to get my permission to test me for drugs.

There's the legal and the medical, I said. I had to know what was going on. If I hadn't found out, you could have died from some little dose of sedative I might prescribe. Secretly, though, I thought she was probably right about the legal stuff. Even so, I realized that no matter how I'd come by it, I was pleased with the clarity we'd achieved.

Rochelle wandered on to those "animal hospitals," as she called them, which sent me reports from time to time:

abscess near her spine arising from God knows where, no one seemed to know; six months' hospitalization for IV antibiotics and pain control; blood infections; spinal fusion . . .

One day she called. I may have to come back to you, she said.

Why?

These fools don't know what they're doing.

My first impulse was to say, as I had before, Sure. Come on back. But my stomach flopped, thinking about the constant arguments over drugs and the load of all that on me and my family.

Only if you're under the care of a pain management center, I said, someone qualified to monitor your narcotics.

David, we're family. We've been together too long not to help each other.

Okay, I said, I'll do your medical care, but you'll have to get your narcotics from someone else. With our history, I just can't do that.

Months later a call came from her doctor. I was giving Mrs. Levinsky her B$_{12}$ shot. I finished my work, said good-bye to Mrs. Levinsky, and turned my attention to the voice on the phone. Rochelle had gotten another infection, waited too long before coming to the hospital. She'd come in nearly comatose. I'm sorry, he said. I couldn't revive her.

First came the shock of her death, then the shock that I was so surprised. I guess I'd really never expected it to happen. She'd always said she was about to die, but it seemed more like a joke we laughed about together than something about to take place in the real world. Now she'd gone and done it.

It made me wonder which was better, the spiky aggravation of having her as a patient or the permanent lament that she might have survived if I'd been there to take care of her. Maybe that had been the source of my predecessor's endurance, staying with her through the smog and stench of drugs so he could be around to pick her up when she fell. Maybe that was the third satisfaction. To endure, so as to save. I couldn't tell. It was what it was. Still swirling in my head was her last visit to my office.

I've told you before, she said, I was not born on this planet. I'm serious. I look around at all these people . . . they have nothing in common with me.

I found myself driving to the ER the other night, David, *alone*. Here I am sick, in pain, and I asked myself, where is *someone* to help me? Do you know what I mean? What is wrong with all these people?

TWO DYINGS

When the retired professor of anthropology came to talk about death, I was not surprised. I knew we'd talk about it sooner or later. He was ninety-three years old. Over the years we had spent more time talking about philosophy and music than about ulcers and prostate cancer. More fun that way. Yet time passes and some things are inevitable. I expected the talk, but what he had to say had an unexpected spin.

It's my wife, he said. The gangrene has set in her leg and she refuses amputation. Absolutely refuses. You see, she has a brother who lost a leg. Just knowing he's there without one leg bothers her so much she can't stand to talk to him. If it came to an operation, she wouldn't do it . . . so . . .

. . . and his words trailed into a shrug. A little seizure formed at the corner of his mouth.

Silence soaked into the minutes ticking.

I remained quiet. The conversation wanted to go where it wanted.

She would have to go first, he said at last. She couldn't do it herself. I'm sure of that. I would have to give it to her . . . then, I guess . . . me.

The last words stuck in his throat like they didn't want to be out in the room.

Ninety-three years is an awfully long time to live, he said. And he raised his eyebrow as I imagined he might in order to drive home an important concept of tribal unity to his anthropology class.

Right then I realized I would do almost anything for this man.

Yet I had no impulse to speak. I wanted to let the idea carry him as far as it wanted.

He asked what would be painless, how much it took to be certain. If he was going to do it, he didn't want to mess up.

We talked about pharmacology and the names of drugs he could have looked up in any neighborhood library. As we talked, I began to see this was not a plan of action but a rehearsal of ideas. The details merely provided something to occupy his voice so his thinking could do its work.

He came to a stopping point. Something had arrived where it needed to arrive, and the silence returned. This time it ebbed from my reluctance to say anything trite or patronizing.

But I was still wondering what I might offer, something

that might give balance to his thinking, give him a little anchor wedged in the rock of this world. It would have to be something automatic, an obligation perhaps, so small as to be unnoticed, so trivial and so easy that *not* to fulfill it would be difficult, something just strong enough to hold him here a little longer. A mark on his calendar, perhaps . . .

 . . . and if I walked out to the front desk and bent over the appointment book with pen in hand and personally wrote down his name . . .

PIANO LESSON

They came flying around us like pigeons I've seen on Parnassus Avenue, domesticated beyond safety among clomping feet and the swift, deadly glide of cars — boys on bicycles, yelling to each other and laughing in that accelerated playful romp that ramps up race-car drivers and athletes, pushing them to take chances.

Duston, my five-year-old son, was in the backseat. We'd just parked our car. We were going to his first piano lesson. He'd wanted to finish listening to *Car Talk* before we went in.

I heard a *thump* sound — no, more like felt it — behind us. The kind of I-hope-it-wasn't-something-bad type of sound we hear occasionally and then go on doing what we were doing before, but with one ear cocked.

We got out of the car and stepped into that recognizable frenzy in the air that rings of danger: someone running, someone stopping their car, a boy in a helmet backing away.

I told Duston to stay by the side of the house and ran

forward, picking up in my sharpening field of vision the crumple of a boy and a bicycle on the pavement, someone leaning over him, blood shining up underneath.

I looked at Duston. He was standing still, looking at me. His hands were over his ears to block out the screams that now were starting from the semiconscious boy on the pavement.

The person leaning over the boy was unsure whether to move him or not. I made a quick assessment: He was conscious, his eyes were open, pupils equal, he was moving all his limbs, trying to pull off his helmet and sit up — probably, I thought, in a desperate attempt to relieve the pain in his head.

I disengaged the bicycle, took the helmet he was handing into space.

Hit and run, someone said. White van. Just kept going.

A lady with a Russian accent came from across the street, bringing a cold wet towel. Place this against his head, she said. Light pressure.

Just light pressure.

I was holding his head, not minding the blood streaming. I worried it might be a sign of skull fracture. I took the towel and placed it on him. The boy pulled it away.

Just light pressure, the Russian lady was saying.

I never know when to identify myself. Now, somehow, it seemed important. I'm a doctor, I said.

Light pressure, she said. Just . . . light. And stepped back.

The boy was restless. It was hard to do anything. I, we,

just contained him in his frantic space, allowing room for him to thrash without injury. He was going to need sedation, and soon.

The fire truck came, the firemen began to do the things they are trained to do: neck brace, head bandage, asking the right questions — what is your name? What day is it today? I noticed his answers were getting less accurate, perhaps from agitation, or pain, or that darker current that runs unseen for a while — deterioration. Everyone was on a cell phone. I was thankful, for once, for the intrusion of technology.

His father arrived and I stepped back. And felt, for the first time, the clench of a sob in my throat. The policeman wanted to know if anyone had gotten a good look at the white van. The Russian lady was standing next to my son, asking who he belonged to and if he shouldn't go home now.

He's mine, I said. And then to Duston, You okay?

Yeah, he said.

I said, It's time to go. And for the first time I had a chance to wonder how this would read out in my son, my son who'd never seen anything like this.

He took my hand, then dropped it. And we realized there was blood all over it. I smiled, wincingly, and then lied a little. I think he's going to be all right, I said.

But the evidence of serious head trauma was written all over him. The boy was starting to show the raccoon eyes that warned of blood welling up somewhere you didn't want to think about. He was confused. I hoped there would be a good neurosurgeon nearby.

I turned to Duston. That's why — and I checked myself.

I know, Dad, he said. That's why you look both ways.

The ambulance drove away. We were back to the lives we had been living, which now would be different. The music teacher asked if we didn't want to postpone. What a way to start, she said.

He's been looking forward to this all week, I said. He's pretty psyched.

Duston nodded.

And, secretly, I thought it was a good thing to return to the ritual we came to perform.

It went well. He and the teacher liked each other. The lesson ran over fifteen minutes. It was hard to turn the key and start up the car when we were done. I drove gingerly, slower by ten miles an hour. It seemed the other drivers were taking too many chances, driving with more insanity than usual. I wondered about full moons, the alignment of stars, phenomena we appeal to when faced with the unfathomable.

The day propelled itself. In the afternoon I called about the boy. Serious but stable, they said. I would call again tomorrow.

In bed that night, I asked my son if he had anything he wanted to talk about. He said no. But I didn't know how much he was thinking about the boy, his mind so filled with peanut butter cookies and the story of Pumpernickel Popcap. I had witnessed his tears, his bravery, to stand within the circle of trauma and say nothing. I'd seen him block out what he could, and deal with what he could not. It was he who discovered the blood, and became neither horrified nor unglued. He knew more than I could tell him if I tried. As for the rest, he would work on it in the mysterious way we all work on horrible things, bringing them up into the light, turning them over and over.

Then putting them back down again, the imprint still with us. Learning to live with that.

PERMISSION ACKNOWLEDGMENTS

"Advance Directive," "Flu Shot," and "Love Is Just a Four-Letter Word" have been previously published in the *Bellevue Literary Review*. "Circus" and "The Girl in the Painting by Vermeer" have been previously published in *Taking the History* (La Plume, Pa.: Nightshade Press, 1999).

National Public Radio's *All Things Considered* has broadcast earlier versions of the following stories: "Circus," "The Doctor with Food on His Shirt," "Evening in the Two Worlds," "Flu Shot," "The Gift of Nothing," "The Girl in the Painting by Vermeer," "Her Language," "Hospital du Jour," "Lunch at the Stereotype Café," and "Piano Lesson."

ABOUT THE AUTHOR

DAVID WATTS, M.D., is a poet and a regular commentator on NPR's *All Things Considered*. He has published three books of poetry and organized the "Writing the Medical Experience" workshops at the Squaw Valley Community of Writers and Sarah Lawrence College. He lives in Mill Valley, California.